Steve —

To a super nice host, even if you don't like
my jerky. I enjoyed being with you
in Houston.
        Karen
                June, 1974

How to Cook His Goose
His Goose
(and Other Wild Games)

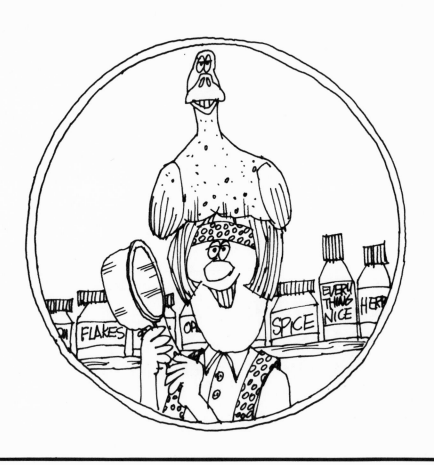

How to Cook His Goose

(and Other Wild Games)

Karen Green and Betty Black

with illustrations by William Green

WINCHESTER PRESS

Library of Congress Catalog Card Number 73-78817
ISBN 0-87691-106-8

Designed by Angela Foote

Published by Winchester Press
460 Park Avenue, New York 10022

Printed in the United States of America

*This book is dedicated to
the greatest sports we know —
Sol and Bill*

Contents

How to Cook His Goose

His Goose
(and Other Wild Games)

For some reason or other, the most confident cook can become apprehensive and uncertain when confronted with a brace of partridge. Even the woman who whips up a perfect soufflé or a divine crêpe may blanch at the prospect of preparing a saddle of venison. We think the whole air of mystery surrounding game cookery, with its vague undertones of difficult preparation, was started by some sportsmen's wives who wanted to keep a good thing to themselves.

Game Cookery:

A Delicious Adventure

Actually, there's nothing mysterious or difficult about cooking game. If you've ever baked a piece of fish in butter, you have mastered the rudiments of preparing Swordfish Steak Meunière. If you've put some chicken pieces into a skillet and added tomato sauce, you're well on your way to a Prairie Chicken Cacciatore.

The best part of game cookery is that your efforts are guaranteed to meet with acclaim from both your sportsman and your guests. There isn't a sportsman alive

3

who wouldn't swear his catch was the greatest he ever tasted. As far as your guests are concerned, they'll be so impressed with eating Rockfish Wellington rather than the usual prime rib bill of fare, you will immediately become a Cook to Be Reckoned With. It will be your secret that the entire dish took only forty minutes from start to serving.

But there's no end to the menu variety a sportsman's wife can produce. All the delicacies that Nature

offers in wild abundance can grace your table, depending on the skill of the hunter. What a relief to be spared the problem of menu boredom! Every cook knows that the same old hamburger in a brand-new sauce still tastes like hamburger in sauce.

Consider the fields and waterways your gourmet supermarket without all the high-priced, fancy foil or plastic-wrapped packages. Nature has her own kind of packaging, and although it may be a little more difficult to unwrap than supermarket fare, even this becomes easy when you know the proper method.

Through this book we would like to show you, step by step, how to prepare your sportsman's catch from cleaning to serving, from basic to more exotic recipes.

We're just wild about game cooking and know you will share our excitement once you learn how to cook his goose and other wild game.

Ask any hunter. He'll agree it's hard to shoot without a gun of some kind. Likewise, a fisherman will tell you it's helpful to have some kind of line and hook. And the more deeply a sportsman becomes involved in his sport, the more likely he'll feel the necessity of adding all kinds of equipment.

In much the same way, it only takes some sort of container and a source of heat to cook the catch, but that's where we separate the "messcooks" from the chefs.

Kitchen
Ammunition

It's all a matter of attitude and pride.

The proper utensil will not only enhance the presentation of your Red Snapper Spinach Pasta, but will make the entire preparation a whole lot easier. Consider it your Kitchen Ammunition.

Your kitchen may already be equipped with many of the utensils we consider indispensable to the game cook. For those items you do not have, we suggest you plan a sporting expedition of your own at your local hardware or department store, gourmet shop, or food market. Splurge a little and purchase the finest quality equipment you can afford. In the long run, the best will provide the greatest economy, since we know that your rewarding experiences in game cookery will require many years of service from your Kitchen Ammunition.

BUCKSHOT
(average price, one dollar)

fish scaler
paraffin
tweezers
heavy-duty foil
freezer paper (coated with cellophane, polyethylene, or wax)
plastic wrap
waxed paper
heavy plastic bags
glass, aluminum, waxed, or rigid plastic containers
marking pen
masking or electrical tape
knife sharpener
assorted wooden spoons
standard measuring cup
cheesecloth
ladle
slotted stainless steel spoon
long-handled fork
can opener
standard measuring spoons
steel tongs
grater

basting brush
basting tube
mixing bowls (assorted sizes)
skewers
heavy-duty trussing thread
tapers (extra-length wooden matches)
potholders
nutcracker
reusable aluminum foil roasting pan
reusable aluminum mousse molds
wire or plastic whisk
fine food strainer
colander

SMALL FIREARMS

(average price, under ten dollars)

poultry shears
pliers
eggbeater
assorted knives
cutting board
wine bottle opener
covered saucepans (1-, 2-, and 3-quart sizes)
covered skillets (8 ½- and 10-inch sizes)
porcelain enamel roasting pan (large size)
covered casserole dishes (assorted sizes)

SNARES AND TRAPS

(Finagle these higher-priced items as his Father's Day gift to you, your birthday gift to him, or in honor of the opening day of hunting and/or fishing seasons.)

covered Dutch ovens (6- and 8-quart sizes)

largest-size electric frypan you can locate
electric mixer
electric blender
heavy-duty cast aluminum covered roasting pan
fish poacher
18-cubic-foot upright freezer*

This may take considerable snaring, trapping, luring, and angling, but it's well worth the effort.

If you've done your Kitchen Ammunition home-work, you're surrounded by all sorts of gadgets . . . knives, tweezers, paraffin, shears, and an eight-quart pot. Set out a big paper or plastic bag for throwaways. Unless you are an apron lover—we are not—we suggest you put on an old pair of slacks and a beat-up top . . . fowl feathers cling. You are now prepared to clean your game birds.

There are three common procedures for removing

A Bird
in the Hand

---

fowl feathers: the dry plucking method, the scalding method, and the paraffin method. Having tried them all, we personally advocate scalding, for the pure and simple reason that it's easier. The dry plucking method needs no explanation.

SCALDING METHOD: First, fill your eight-quart pot with water and put it on to boil. While the water is boiling, cut the throat of the bird and hang the head to bleed. (Aren't you glad you're wearing old slacks!) This bleeding process is technically referred to as "drawing."

Once your water has come to a boil, turn off the heat and allow the water to cool for a few minutes. Holding the bird by its feet, dip it in the scalding water repeatedly until the feathers are completely soaked. A small bird, such as a grouse, will require about two minutes of dunking and swishing around, while a larger bird, a pheasant, for instance, may take four minutes to ensure a complete soaking of feathers. Don't get overzealous with the scalding. The idea is to loosen the feathers, not to make soup. Also, overscalding can loosen the skin so that it may slip off. A skinned bird may lose eye appeal and taste appeal in the final preparation.

You can now accomplish the de-feathering process quite easily. Take just a small tuft of feathers at a time and gently pluck toward the direction of the tail.

Since the feathers of a duck or goose (both are waterfowl) are naturally well-oiled, they come out fairly easily using the dry plucking method, which simply means plucking out a few feathers at a time in the direction of the tail. However, here again, you may find that scalding expedites the plucking operation.

Keeping in mind that the natural oils in duck or goose feathers tend to make the water slip off their surface, we suggest ruffling up the feathers before scalding so the hot water can penetrate to the skin.

The paraffin method of plucking waterfowl is most popular among master chefs. This method is considerably more tricky than the dry plucking method since the melted wax hardens fast. If you wish to experiment, here's how:

PARAFFIN METHOD: Have an eight-quart pot of boiling water ready on the stove. Shave in a couple of pounds of paraffin and let it melt. Cut off the bird's wings and feet, since you will not want to eat them anyway. Using the head as a handle, dip the bird several times so that it becomes well coated with wax. Allow the paraffin to cool and harden, then scrape it off with a dull knife. The down and pinfeathers should come off with the paraffin. Any remaining pinfeathers can be singed off with a lighted roll of newspaper or plucked out with tweezers.

Whether dry-plucked, scalded, or paraffin-plucked, your bird is now ready for eviscerating.

TO EVISCERATE: Place bird on its back and slit the skin over the crop to remove it. (The crop is a sac-like enlargement of the throat in which the bird's food is

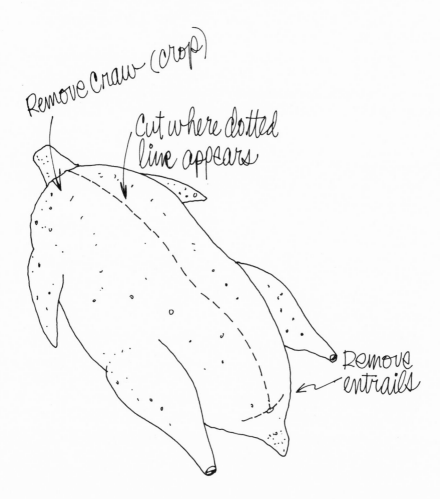

softened for digestion.) Make a second incision across the bird, starting to the rear of the breastbone and around the vent (see illustration). This allows for the easy removal of all entrails—large intestine, heart, lungs, liver, kidneys, gizzard, and windpipe. Thrust your fingers deep inside the neck to remove the "quacker" or voice box.

All entrails must be completely removed, including the red, spongy lung bits which may put up a fight for survival by adhering to the ribs. Separate the giblets (heart, liver, and gizzard) and save for the stuffing, sauce, or a wild pâté.

The empty cavity should be cleaned thoroughly. Remove any pellets or blood clots. Then wash the bird thoroughly with cold water, pat dry with paper towels, and sprinkle the cavity with salt.

In many cases, particularly with dove and pigeon, it is best to "breast out" your bird.

TO BREAST OUT: Snap off both wing bones as close as you can to the body. Discard. Pick the feathers from the breast to expose the ridge of the breastbone. Using your thumbs, place one thumb on each side of the ridge. Press the skin back with your thumbs (skin will part). Now, stick one thumb into the cavity below the breast. Lift the breast right out. Discard remaining parts.

There are two schools of thought concerning the handling of game birds after the kill. Some people feel they should be "hung" (aged) *before* plucking and drawing. Others feel they should be aged *after* cleaning. The followers of both schools have a host of arguments supporting their particular belief. We suggest cleaning first because it is easier and also prevents your kitchen or refrigerator from taking on a gamy aroma.

Since not too many of us have easy access to a butcher's walk-in, game aging is best done in the refrigerator, where the temperature is controlled.

TO AGE: After cleaning, place birds in a bowl or pan so any remaining blood will not drip all over the groceries, cover with plastic wrap, and refrigerate for one to three days before cooking or freezing. This short aging process tenderizes the birds and gives them extra flavor. Allow two or three days for duck, pheasant, and chukar, and one or two days for grouse, quail, dove, and pigeon. Wild geese need not be aged.

Many of the above steps may have been done by your sportsman and his friends during the hunt. If so, he has "field-stripped" the bird. Impress him with your knowledgeability by suggesting he stuff the cleaned cavity with fresh-cut grass so that air will easily circulate and keep the bird fresh.

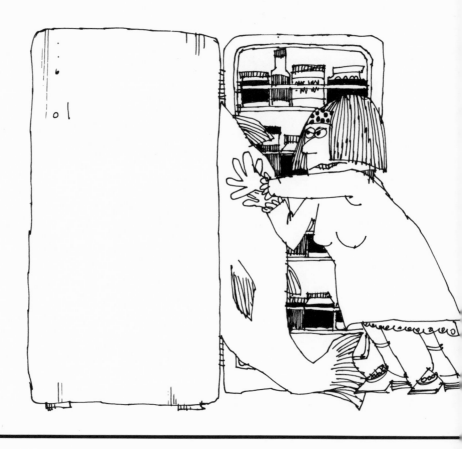

Even if you are planning to cook some of the dressed game at once, you will want to freeze the remainder. Three cheers for our modern-day kitchen conveniences. With the help of your knight in shining white porcelain you can delight your family with wild duck two months after the season has closed.

Much of your success with the freezer section of your refrigerator—or, if you are fortunate enough to own one, your giant home freezer unit—depends upon how you

A Game
Attempt
at Freezing

package, wrap, and seal the game. Everything must be protected against the dry, cold air so that your food will not develop off-flavors or lose color, moisture, and nutritive value.

For your foray into the frigid zone, arm yourself with aluminum foil (not the common household variety but the super-strength broiler type), freezer paper coated with cellophane, polyethylene, or wax, good-quality plastic bags, and waxed cartons. Make sure these cartons are heavy-duty and moisture- and vapor-proof. Don't be chintzy and try to use ordinary ice cream, cottage cheese, or milk cartons; they do not provide adequate protection. You may also need glass, pottery, aluminum, or rigid plastic containers for freezing fish. A marking pen and masking or heavy electrical tape will complete your equipment.

Now let us consider what you are about to freeze. If the food at hand is small, such as dove and quail or fish fillets and steaks, you may want to package a few together (of the same item, of course) for individual serving portions. However, put only as much in a single freezer package as you can use in one meal.

Place two sheets of plastic or other moisture-and vapor-proof wrap between each bird or fish; otherwise, the pieces will freeze into a solid block. Once you have taken this precaution, the freezing steps are the same as for larger game.

Use your freezer foil or plastic see-through wrap for the first layer, taking care to mold it close to the food to exclude air. Next, wrap it tightly with freezer paper and seal the turned ends of the package with tape.

If you wish, fillets, steaks, or small whole fish can be packed in rigid containers. Fill the open spaces with cold water, snap on the top of the container, and cover with freezer wrap. All fat (oily fleshed) fish, such as barracuda, hold best if frozen in ice. We do not suggest freezing birds in this manner, for you may drown their delicate flavor . . . fish are at home in this watery habitat.

Immediately after wrapping, every package should be clearly labeled to indicate contents, portion, and date of freezing. Put the label where you will be able to read it without unwrapping the package. Don't trust your memory. If you invite guests for Albacore with Chili Peppers, you do not want to surprise them — or yourself — with Canadian Honkers Olé!

When you put the packages in the freezer for final

storage, try to arrange them according to category, reserving separate sections for fish, fowl, and meat. Or, if
you own a standing upright freezer, reserve a level for
each different catch; this will enable you to find what
you want with a minimum of fumbling or hoisting heavy
packages around while your freezer defrosts.

Now that we have all your game neatly packaged
and stored for future use, the next important point to
consider is proper defrosting. Of course, the occasion
may arise when you'll be called upon to perform game
cooking magic on very short notice. (A proud husband
may call you at five o'clock to impress his boss at seven.)
Out of necessity, it is possible to cook poultry and fish
while still in the frozen state. However, under normal
circumstances, proper defrosting will definitely provide
a much more uniform cooking and the desired degree of
doneness.

The golden rule to remember when defrosting is
"The slower the better." This way the food will retain
most of its natural moisture.

There are two methods of defrosting: the defrost-in-
the-refrigerator method and the defrost-at-room-temper-

ature method. According to our personal experience, defrosting at room temperature, while producing faster results, requires a little more care. If your household should include domestic pets, we suggest you avoid the hazard of your dog running off with your dinner by selecting a defrosting spot high out of his reach. If you happen to own a cat, put the cat out before you take your prospective dinner out!

For fowl, allow five to six hours per pound in the refrigerator and two to three hours per pound at room temperature. This timetable works for meat, too.

For fish, allow an average of six to ten hours in the refrigerator and three hours per pound at room temperature, depending upon thickness. (A half-inch-thick two-pound steak will defrost faster than a two-inch-thick two-pound fillet, for example. Especially during warm weather, we suggest defrosting in your refrigerator to prevent possible spoilage.

When you need to hasten the thawing of fish, place the wrapped package in a colander under cold running water to drain as it thaws. Thawed fish should be used immediately.

Never refreeze game in its original state. However, it is safe to cook the game and then freeze the finished product.

Here is a table of maximum freezer storage time for your uncooked game:

Fowl   6 to 8 months
Fish
   Fat (oily fleshed)   4 to 6 months
     (albacore, barracuda, mahimahi, pompano, salmon)
   Lean   6 to 8 months
     (bonito, halibut, lingcod, red snapper, rockfish, sea bass, swordfish, trout)

Meat   6 to 8 months
(Edible organs such as heart and liver should
be used within 6 months.)

By adhering to these simple suggestions, your trophies will be protected against freezer burn and will maintain all their natural juices and flavors.

Any meal can become a festive occasion when game birds are on the menu.

UPLAND GAME BIRDS

Upland game birds, such as pheasant, chukar, prairie chicken, quail, dove, and pigeon, live off the fat of the

A Feather in Your Cap

land. Their diet features various seeds, grains, fruits, and nuts, making them fine eating. The younger, the more juicy; however, you will find that certain recipes using moist heat (as in stewing), casserole dishes with sauces, and dishes calling for marinades will turn an old bird into a "spring chicken." After you have tested these recipes, you may wish to experiment by substituting one bird for another.

Baked Pheasant in Skim Milk

1 pheasant, cleaned
Salt and pepper
4 tablespoons butter

1 cup your favorite
stuffing
1 quart skim milk

Prepare whole pheasant as you would a domestic turkey. Rub the bird with salt and pepper. Sauté the whole bird in butter until it is a light golden color. Stuff the cavity with your favorite dressing, skewer it closed, and place it in a roaster. Add the skim milk. Bake in a 325- to 350-degree oven, 30 minutes per pound, basting about every 10 minutes with the liquid.

For stuffing, try chopping the pheasant heart, liver, and gizzard. Sauté them with chopped onions, celery, and red and green peppers. Mix with sage and cooked wild rice.

Serves 2 to 3.

Pheasant Simmered with Apples

1 pheasant, cleaned and
cut into serving pieces
4 tablespoons butter
Salt and pepper
2 Golden Delicious

apples, peeled, cored,
and cut into large
chunks
1 tablespoon cinnamon
1 cup apple cider

Melt the butter in a casserole, then add the pheasant. Sprinkle with salt and pepper. Brown the bird all over for about 8 minutes. Add the apples, cinnamon, and apple cider. Cover and simmer for about 1 hour, or until the pheasant is tender.

Serves 2 to 3.

Pheasant Teriyaki

1 young pheasant, split

Teriyaki Marinade:

4 tablespoons butter
3/4 tablespoon grated
   ginger root (or 1/3
   teaspoon powdered
   ginger)

1/3 cup soy sauce
2 tablespoons sugar
1/4 cup white wine
1 clove garlic

Lightly brown the pheasant in butter and then place it in a shallow pan. Combine the remaining ingredients and pour the marinade over the pheasant. Marinate for 1 hour in the refrigerator.

Place each pheasant half on a large piece of heavy-duty aluminum foil, cover with marinade, and seal foil at the top and ends. Wrap each half with a second piece of foil. Place in a shallow pan or pie tin to catch any juice that might escape. Roast at 325 degrees for 1 1/4 hours.

This marinade is also good for barbecuing pheasant.

Serves 2.

Pheasant in Sour Cream

1 pheasant, cleaned and
   cut into serving pieces
Flour
4 tablespoons butter
2 tablespoons fresh
   chopped onion

Salt and pepper
1 cup sour cream
2 sprigs parsley, chopped

Dredge the pheasant in flour. Melt the butter in a large skillet, then sauté the pheasant with the onion. Sprinkle with salt and pepper. Transfer all the ingredients to a baking dish. Blanket with sour cream and parsley.

Cover the dish and bake at 350 degrees for about 1½ hours. The sour cream will tenderize the meat.

Serves 2 to 3.

Rosemary's Pheasant

2 pheasant, cleaned and
   cut into serving pieces
4 tablespoons olive oil
3 garlic cloves, sliced
Salt and pepper to taste

1 tablespoon rosemary
   (preferably fresh)
⅓ cup wine vinegar (you
   may substitute dry
   sherry)

Wash, drain, but do not dry the pheasant pieces. In a large skillet lightly brown the garlic in olive oil. Add the pheasant and season with salt, pepper, and rosemary. Cover and simmer slowly for about 1 hour, or until the meat appears tender when tested with a fork. But check occasionally; if the meat appears dry, add about ½ cup water. When done, add the vinegar. Turn off the heat. Cover again and let steam for 5 minutes. When serving, pour the cooking juices over the pheasant.

Serves 4 to 6.

Pheasant in Cream Sauce

1 pheasant, cleaned and
   dressed
Salt and pepper to taste
¼ pound (½ cup) butter
   (plus additional butter)

3 tablespoons flour
½ cup cold milk
½ cup crushed cracker
   crumbs

Place the pheasant in a Dutch oven with 2 cups of hot water, cover, and put into a 375-degree oven. After 1/2 hour, season with salt and pepper and continue to cook until the meat falls from the bones. Remove the bones and skin and place the pheasant meat on a hot ovenproof platter. Put aside.

Melt 1/4 pound butter in a pan. Stir in the flour until it is smoothly blended. Slowly add the cold milk, stirring until the sauce thickens. Add the stock from the cooked pheasant to the pan. Season with additional salt and pepper to taste. Pour the sauce over the meat on the platter. Sprinkle with crushed cracker crumbs, dot with butter, and return to the oven until the butter melts.

Serves 2 to 3.

Pheasant Rice Supreme in Foil

2 pheasant, cleaned
3 tablespoons bacon
  drippings
5 tablespoons butter
1 cup brown or wild rice
4-ounce can sliced
  mushrooms, drained
1/2 teaspoon salt

1/4 teaspoon ground
  ginger
3 cups chicken broth or
  bouillon
1 large onion, quartered
1 stalk celery with leaves,
  cut into large pieces
Flour

Disjoint the pheasant. Set aside the backs, wings, and necks. Brown the remainder in the bacon drippings combined with 3 tablespoons of the butter.

Cook the rice according to the package directions.

Brown the mushrooms in the remaining butter. Add them to the rice. Mix in the salt and ginger. Place the rice mixture on a large piece of heavy-duty aluminum foil and top with the pheasant pieces. Seal the foil. Bake in a 350-degree oven for approximately 1½ hours. Open the foil and bake for another 15 minutes.

To make gravy: In a saucepan combine the pheasant backs, wings, and necks, chicken broth, onion, and celery. Bring to a boil, reduce the heat, and simmer for approximately 30 minutes. Strain the liquid. Add flour until the desired gravy consistency is achieved. Season to taste.

Serves 4.

There's nothing more posh than baked pheasant and champagne for a picnic. It's as easy to do as baked or fried chicken. It just has a bit more flair.

Picnic Pheasant

2 pheasant, cleaned and
cut into serving pieces
2 eggs, lightly beaten
(add salt and pepper to
taste)

2 cups favorite seasoned
bread crumbs (Italian
style, country style)
Cooking oil

Dip the pheasant pieces into the egg mixture. Pour the bread crumbs into a plastic or paper bag. Drop in one pheasant piece at a time and shake it around in the bag. Place the pieces on a greased baking sheet. Bake in a 375-degree oven for about 45 minutes to 1 hour, or until tender. Allow to cool. Wrap for a picnic.

Serves 4 to 6.

German-Style Pheasant with Sauerkraut

2 pheasant, halved
8 new potatoes, peeled
4 carrots, scraped and cut
  into thirds
½ cup butter
6 strips bacon
27-ounce can sauerkraut,
  drained

1 teaspoon caraway seeds
½ teaspoon cracked black
  pepper
¼ cup dry white wine
  (Sauterne)

Parboil the new potatoes and carrot chunks in separate pots for about 10 minutes. Immediately drain so that the vegetables do not continue to cook, then set them aside. Brown the pheasant halves in butter until they are golden. Remove the pheasant from the skillet. In the same skillet, fry 2 strips of the bacon to render fat but remove the bacon before it is crisp. Roll the carrots and potatoes in some of the pan drippings for flavor. Set aside again.

In a large mixing bowl, combine the sauerkraut, caraway seeds, cracked pepper, remaining pan drippings, and wine. Tear the 2 strips of cooked bacon into small pieces, add to the mixture, and combine thoroughly.

Place half of the sauerkraut mixture in the bottom of a large casserole and top with the pheasant halves. Surround the pheasant with the remaining sauerkraut. Place the potatoes and carrots around the pheasant. Cover each bird half with 1 strip of bacon. Cover the casserole. Bake at 350 degrees for 45 minutes, occasionally basting the birds and vegetables with the pan drippings. Uncover and bake for another 30 minutes. Continue to baste. The bacon imparts a rich flavor to all the ingredients.

Serves 4.

Pheasant Creole

3 pheasant, cleaned and
   cut into serving pieces
¾ cup flour
2 teaspoons paprika
2 teaspoons salt
¾ teaspoon pepper
¼ cup butter
½ teaspoon ground basil

1 cup white wine
8-ounce can tomato sauce
4-ounce can sliced
   mushrooms (retain
   liquid)
3 green peppers, sliced
1 medium onion, sliced
¼ cup cornstarch

Combine the flour, paprika, 1 teaspoon of the salt, and ¼ teaspoon of the pepper. Roll the pheasant pieces in the flour mixture and then brown them in the butter. Add the remaining salt and pepper, basil, wine, tomato sauce, and mushroom liquid. Cover and simmer for 10 minutes, or until sauce is bubbly.

Stir in the mushrooms, green peppers, and onion. Cook for 10 minutes, or until the onion is soft. Cover and cook over low heat for another 30 minutes, or until the pheasant is tender. Remove the pheasant pieces to a hot platter.

Combine the cornstarch with half a cup of cold water and stir it into the pan juices. Heat and stir until the sauce is thickened. Pour it over the pheasant.

Serves 6 to 8.

A tasty way to prepare leftovers.

Pheasant Rarebit

1 cup cooked leftover
   pheasant (small pieces)
½ cup condensed
   Cheddar cheese soup

½ cup beer
1 teaspoon
   Worcestershire sauce
½ teaspoon dry mustard

Combine the soup, beer, Worcestershire sauce, and dry mustard and stir until completely smooth and blended. Pour the mixture into a saucepan; add the pheasant pieces. Heat at moderate temperature for 10 minutes, stirring occasionally. Serve hot over toast points or toasted English muffins.

If you do not have a full cup of leftover pheasant, you can make up the difference by adding cooked, crumbled bacon.

Serves 2.

Pickled Pheasant

2 pheasant, cleaned and
   skinned
Salt
1 cup vinegar (plus
   additional to taste)

1 package pickling spices
3 bay leaves
1 medium onion, sliced

Cut up the pheasant as you would for frying. Place the pieces in a 6-quart kettle. Add water until meat is three-fourths covered. Salt well and add 1 cup vinegar. Slowly bring to a simmer. Simmer until half-done. (To test, pierce with a fork; some blood should appear.)

At the halfway point, add more vinegar. Taste the broth, adding vinegar, until it reaches the degree of sourness you desire. Continually add water to keep the bird three-fourths covered, since some of the water will evaporate. Add the package of pickling spices, bay leaves, and onion slices.

Continue to simmer for about an hour longer until the pheasant is completely done. When cooked, the liquid will jell somewhat. Keep in the refrigerator.

Breast of Pheasant Vodka

4 large pheasant breasts
6 mushrooms, finely
  chopped
½ pound (1 cup) plus 4
  tablespoons butter
1 clove garlic, finely
  minced

2 tablespoons chopped
  parsley
Salt and pepper
2 eggs
1 tablespoon vodka
Fine bread crumbs

Remove all the bones and skin from 4 large pheasant breasts. Cut each breast in half, making 8 pieces. Place each half breast between 2 sheets of waxed paper and flatten it with the flat side of a cleaver or wooden mallet until it somewhat resembles a pancake.

Sauté the finely chopped mushrooms in 1 tablespoon of the butter for about 5 minutes.

Let ½ pound of the butter come to room temperature. Then cream together the butter with the garlic, parsley, and sautéed mushrooms. Chill in the refrigerator until firm enough to handle. Then shape the seasoned butter into 8 oval rolls about 2½ to 3 inches long and ¾ to 1 inch wide at the thickest part. Place these rolls into cold water with ice cubes in it and let them remain until hard.

Sprinkle each flattened breast of pheasant with salt and pepper. Remove butter rolls from the ice water, dry each quickly, and place one roll on each of the flattened breasts. Roll the pheasant around the butter roll, folding the ends in so that the butter rolls are completely encased. Secure the rolled pheasant with wooden toothpicks.

Lightly beat the eggs with the vodka. Roll the breasts in bread crumbs, then in the beaten eggs and vodka and then again in the bread crumbs.

Fry in plenty of butter until the rolls are goldenbrown, making certain that the butter is not too hot. (You don't want the ouside to completely brown before the pheasant is thoroughly cooked.) When the rolls are golden-brown, drain on paper toweling and place in a hot oven for about 5 minutes. Serve immediately.

Serves 8.

Phractured Pheasant

1 pheasant, cleaned
2 strips bacon
6-ounce jar currant jelly

Fruit and Nut Stuffing:
6-ounce package dried
   mixed fruits
1/4 cup pecan halves
1 green apple, peeled,
   cored, and chopped
Lemon juice
1 egg, beaten

1/2 cup butter
1 cup bourbon

1/3 cup brown sugar,
   packed
1 tablespoon cinnamon
1/3 cup croutons
1/4 cup grated Parmesan
   cheese

Soak the dried fruit for 15 minutes in water which has been brought to a boil. Drain and combine with the pecans, apple pieces which have been sprinkled with lemon juice, egg, sugar, cinnamon, croutons, cheese, and enough water to moisten.

Rinse the pheasant thoroughly and pat it dry. Stuff with the Fruit and Nut Stuffing and sew or skewer openings. Place the pheasant in a baking pan. Cover with the bacon strips to keep breast moist while roasting. Melt the jelly with the butter in a small pan and blend well. Use this mixture to baste the bird. Roast the pheasant, uncovered, in a 350-degree oven for 1 to 1 1/2 hours. Add the bourbon to the pan glaze during last 15 minutes. Baste frequently.

Serves 2 to 3.

This is an ideal way to prepare an old pheasant, one that has been badly shot, or one that has been slightly freezer-burned, because the creamy sauce will tenderize the meat.

Pheasant Stroganoff

1 small pheasant, cleaned, cut into serving pieces and skinned
2 cups milk
2 tablespoons butter
Salt and pepper, onion and garlic powder to taste
10 3/4-ounce can condensed cream of mushroom soup
3 1/2-ounce can whole button mushrooms, drained
1/2 cup sherry
2 teaspoons paprika
1/2 cup sour cream

Soak the pheasant in milk for 4 hours. Pat dry. Melt the butter and sauté the pheasant in a large skillet until all sides are lightly browned. Sprinkle with salt, pepper, onion and garlic powder to taste. Add the mushroom soup and mushrooms and stir. Add ¼ cup of the sherry. Stir again, covering the pheasant with sauce. Sprinkle paprika over the sauce. Cover and simmer for 45 minutes. Uncover and add the remaining ¼ cup sherry. Stir well. Remove the pheasant to a hot serving platter. Add the sour cream to the sauce, stir, and spoon the sauce on top of the pheasant.

Serves 2.

Leftover pheasant can make a marvelous cocktail or sandwich spread.

Pheasant Spread

Leftover pheasant (from any of the previous recipes)
Salt, pepper, and vinegar to taste

Take leftover *cold* pheasant and pick off all the meat. Wings and legs are the best meat for this dish. Finely chop the pheasant and put it in a saucepan with water to cover. Add salt and pepper to taste and a small amount of vinegar. Bring to a boil and boil for 5 minutes. Take it off the heat and let it sit for a few minutes. It can be eaten now or put up in jars or cans. Or it will keep in your refrigerator for 10 days to 2 weeks. Delicious on rye bread.

Pheasant Pâté

½ cup pheasant livers
2 tablespoons butter
1 small shallot bulb,
  finely diced
¼ teaspoon salt

¼ teaspoon pepper
¼ teaspoon dry mustard
2 tablespoons Marsala
  wine
1 raw egg yolk

Melt the butter in a skillet. Add the shallot, salt, pepper, and dry mustard and sauté until shallot is soft. Add the livers and wine and sauté the livers until done (approximately 3 minutes each side), turning constantly to keep the livers from sticking to the pan. Place the entire mixture, including pan drippings, in an electric blender container. Add the raw egg yolk. Turn on the blender and puree the mixture. Chill until served. This will keep well in your refrigerator for 3 to 4 days.

If you do not have an electric blender, dice the livers in a small bowl, add the egg yolk and pan drippings, and mix. Hold a fine strainer over a bowl and place only a small amount of the liver mixture into strainer at a time. Mash the mixture with the back of a spoon, forcing it through the strainer into the bowl. Be sure to scrape off the pâté that clings to the outside of the strainer. Repeat the procedure until the pâté is done. Chill as above.

Wild Game Pâté

½ cup game bird livers,
  preferably pheasant or
  goose
1 green onion (scallion)
  bulb, sliced as thinly as
  possible
2 medium-size fresh
  mushrooms, chopped

2 tablespoons butter,
  melted
2 tablespoons dry sherry
¼ teaspoon
  Worcestershire sauce
Salt, pepper, and
  garlic powder

Sauté the livers with the green onion and mushrooms in melted butter for approximately 6 minutes,
frequently turning the livers. Add 1 tablespoon of the
sherry while sautéing. If an electric blender is available,
place the cooked mixture in the container and puree until it becomes the consistency of paste. Otherwise, mash
the livers by pushing them through a fine strainer with
the back of a spoon. Add the remaining tablespoon of
sherry and the Worcestershire sauce. Season to taste. If
too dry, add a small amount of melted butter.

Form into a ball and chill. Delicious as a party hors
d'oeuvre with crackers or rye rounds. Keeps beautifully
in the refrigerator for several days.

Chukar has a delicate meat similar in flavor and texture to pheasant. From the South comes this interesting stuffing variation.

Dixieland Roasted Chukar

1 chukar, cleaned	½ cup cornbread
¾ cup melted butter	½ cup stale baker's bread
Salt and pepper	2 small onions

Wipe the chukar cavity with a damp cloth. Brush it inside and out with melted butter. Sprinkle with salt and pepper. In a bowl, break up the cornbread and stale baker's bread. Moisten bread mixture with ¼ cup of the melted butter. Peel and chop the onions. Sauté them in 1 tablespoon melted butter until brown. Add the onions to the bread mixture and combine thoroughly. Season to taste with salt and pepper.

Stuff and truss the bird. Place in a moderately hot oven (375 degrees) and roast for 1 hour. Baste frequently with the drippings and melted butter.

Serves 2.

Roast Chukar with Rice Stuffing

4 chukar, cleaned
¼ cup butter

Brown or Wild Rice Stuffing:

1 cup packaged brown or wild rice	mushrooms (drain and retain liquid)
1 medium onion finely chopped	¼ cup butter
½ cup diced celery with celery leaves	1 teaspoon salt
4-ounce can sliced	½ teaspoon ground marjoram
	⅛ teaspoon pepper

Prepare the stuffing first: Cook the rice for 5 minutes less than the package directions call for. Set aside. Sauté the onion, celery, and mushrooms in butter until tender and then add them to the rice. Mix in salt, marjoram, and pepper. Add the mushroom liquid as needed. The mixture should be moist and should hold together very well. Lightly spoon the stuffing into the birds.

Wrap each chukar separately in heavy-duty aluminum foil. Roast at 325 degrees for 1 hour. Unwrap the birds and brush them with butter. Increase the oven temperature to 425 degrees and continue roasting for 10 to 15 minutes, or until the birds are brown.

Serves 8.

Chukar Partridge in Wine

4 whole partridge breasts
1 onion, sliced into thin rings
1 stalk celery, chopped
½ teaspoon dried tarragon
1 cup white wine
6 tablespoons butter

4 tablespoons flour
½ teaspoon salt
Dash of pepper
1 egg yolk, slightly beaten
4 tablespoons heavy cream

Cut the breasts in half along the breastbone. Pull off the skin. Place the breasts, onion, celery, tarragon, and wine in a large saucepan. Add just enough water to cover the breasts. Cover and simmer for 30 minutes.

Remove the breasts and keep them warm. Strain the liquid, then boil and reduce it to 2 cups. Melt 4 tablespoons of the butter and stir in the flour, salt, and pepper. Gradually add the partridge broth.

Stir constantly until the mixture is smooth and thickened. Add the remaining butter and simmer gently for 5 minutes. In a small bowl, combine the egg yolk and cream and add to the sauce. Stir and pour the sauce on top of the partridge breasts.

Serve on toast triangles with brandied or minted pears.

Serves 6 to 8.

Stuffed Chukar Stroganoff

3 chukar
1 cup Brown or Wild
  Rice Stuffing (*see* page
  40)
6 tablespoons flour
1 teaspoon salt
½ teaspoon poultry
  seasoning

¼ teaspoon pepper
½ cup butter
1 onion, quartered
4-ounce can sliced
  mushrooms (retain
  liquid)
⅔ cups dry red wine
1 pint sour cream

Stuff the chukar with Brown or Wild Rice Stuffing. Tie the legs close to the body. Combine 2 tablespoons of the flour with the salt, poultry seasoning, and pepper. Sprinkle lightly over the chukar. Melt the butter in a large frypan, add the birds, and brown them slowly; it should take 25 to 30 minutes. Place the chukar in a Dutch oven or earthenware casserole. Add the drippings, onion, mushrooms, and wine. Cover. Bake in a 350-degree oven for 45 minutes, or until tender. Remove the birds to a hot platter.

Stir the sour cream into the pan drippings. Heat and add as much of the remaining flour as necessary to achieve the desired sauce thickness. Season to taste. Spoon the sauce over the chukar. Serve immediately.

Serves 6.

A garden of herbs gives a marvelous flavor and aroma to this dish.

Savory Baked Prairie Chicken

1 prairie chicken, cleaned
¼ cup flour
½ teaspoon salt
¼ teaspoon pepper
½ teaspoon savory

¼ cup milk
Dash of thyme and basil
1 strip bacon
1 tablespoon butter

Combine the flour, salt, pepper, and savory. Dip the bird in milk and then dredge in the flour mixture. Sprinkle thyme and basil on the bacon, roll it up, and place it in the body cavity. Close the opening with toothpicks. Melt the butter in a skillet and then brown the bird. Remove the bird and place it in a baking dish, cover, and bake in 325-degree oven for 1 hour, or until tender. Check occasionally; if the skin appears too dry, baste with additional melted butter.

Serves 2 to 4.

Curried Prairie Chicken

2 prairie chickens,
   breasted out (*see* page
   16)
¼ cup flour
¼ teaspoon pepper
¼ teaspoon paprika
4 tablespoons butter

1 onion, diced
¼ teaspoon salt
1 tablespoon curry
   powder
1 cup chicken broth (or
   bouillon)

Split the breasts; remove the fillets. Cut the breast fillets into bite-size pieces. Put flour, pepper, and paprika in a paper bag, add the prairie chicken pieces, and shake until all are well coated with flour mixture. Melt the butter in a large frypan and sauté the flour-coated breast pieces lightly on each side; then remove them from the pan. In same frypan, sauté the onion until soft; add the salt, curry powder, and chicken broth. If the liquid is thin, blend in ½ tablespoon of the flour mixture (from the paper bag) to thicken. Return the breast pieces to the pan, lower the heat, and cover. Simmer for 20 minutes, stirring occasionally. Remove the cover and simmer for 5 minutes more, or until the breast pieces are done.

Serve with bowls of hot white rice and condiments such as chutney, raisins, chopped peanuts, coconut, and sliced banana.

Serves 4 to 5.

Prairie Chicken Cacciatore

3 whole prairie chicken breasts (on bone)
Salt and pepper
1 stalk celery, cut into chunks
1 raw carrot, cut into pieces
3 tablespoons cooking oil
1 onion, diced
3 green peppers, cut into large pieces (remove seeds and membrane)
½ teaspoon garlic powder

15-ounce can tomato sauce
1 teaspoon Worcestershire sauce
1 cup dry red wine
1 cup sautéed sliced mushrooms
16-ounce can whole peeled tomatoes
¼ cup grated Parmesan cheese

Sprinkle the prairie chicken breasts with salt and pepper, place in a sauce pot with the celery, carrot, and enough water to just cover the breasts. Bring the water to a boil, reduce the heat to a simmer, and cover the pot. Allow the breasts to simmer for approximately 30 minutes, or until fork-tender. Remove the breasts from the liquid, place them on a platter, and let them cool. When they are cool enough to handle, remove the skin and carefully separate each breast fillet from the bone. This will give you six breast fillets.

Pour the cooking oil into a large saucepan or chicken fryer. Add the onion, green pepper, and garlic powder, and sauté until soft; then push the vegetables to the side of the pan. Add the breast fillets in a single layer, quickly sautéing them on each side until they are a light golden color. (Add a little more cooking oil if needed.) Reduce the heat to a simmer and add the tomato sauce, Worcestershire sauce, and ⅓ cup of the wine. Stir all the ingredients so that the onion and green pepper are spread over the breast fillets. Reduce the heat, cover, and let simmer for 15 minutes. Add the mushrooms, whole tomatoes, Parmesan cheese, and another ⅓ cup wine. Stir through, cover, and continue to simmer for 10 more minutes. Just before serving, add the remaining wine and sprinkle with a little more Parmesan cheese as garnish. Serve with a salad and hot white rice.

Serves 6.

Texan-Style Sweet Potatoes and Prairie Chicken

2 prairie chickens,
  skinned and breasted
  out (*see* page 16)
4 medium sweet potatoes
  or yams
½ cup milk
½ cup cornflake crumbs
Salt and pepper

3 tablespoons butter
1 cup orange juice
¼ cup dry sherry
1 bouillon cube
½ teaspoon ginger
1 teaspoon brown sugar
½ cup pecan halves

Boil the sweet potatoes in their skins in a covered saucepan for 5 minutes. Drain, rinse in cold water, peel, and halve each one lengthwise. Set the potatoes aside.

Cut prairie chicken breasts in half lengthwise down the bone. Wipe with a damp paper towel. Dip the chicken in milk and then coat with the cornflake crumbs. Sprinkle with salt and pepper. Melt the butter in a skillet and brown the chicken on both sides; it will take about 8 minutes. Remove the chicken from the heat.

In a Pyrex baking dish, combine the pan drippings, orange juice, sherry, bouillon cube, ginger, and brown sugar and stir thoroughly. Arrange the chicken breasts and sweet potatoes in the sauce. Sprinkle with the pecan halves. Cover and bake at 350 degrees for 1 hour, or until tender.

Serves 4 to 6.

Prairie Chicken Roulades

2 prairie chicken breasts
2 teaspoons prepared
  mustard
2 thin strips bacon
3 carrots, scraped and cut
  into thin strips
  (lengthwise)
2 celery stalks, cut into
  thin strips (lengthwise)

1 medium onion, cut into
  thin rings
½ cup butter
2 tomatoes, quartered
10¾-ounce can
  condensed cream of
  mushroom soup
Salt and pepper

Split the prairie chicken breasts and remove all the bones; this will give you four fillets. On a cutting board or any hard surface, place a double sheet of waxed paper, one fillet, and another double layer of waxed paper. Pound the fillet to ¼ inch thickness. If the top layer of waxed paper should break, replace with more. Repeat the process with the other three fillets.

On each fillet, spread ½ teaspoon of prepared mustard, then layer lengthwise ½ strip of bacon and widthwise, alternately, a few carrot and celery stalks. Top with 2 thin onion rings. Roll the fillets carefully, so as not to lose any stuffing. Secure all the openings with tooth-picks. Individually brown each rollup in melted butter, turning to make certain all the ends are golden, then remove the rollup from the pan. Pour the pan drippings into a Pyrex casserole. Add the rollups, tomato quarters, and soup. Cover and bake at 350 degrees for 45 minutes. Check once and spoon the liquid on top of the rollups.

Prior to serving, remove the toothpicks. Serve on top of plenty of fluffy white rice.

Serves 3 to 4.

A delicious, hearty meal-in-one-pot specialty that has been in our family for four generations is

Jean's Stewed Prairie Chicken with Dumplings

1 prairie chicken, cleaned
2 stalks celery, cut into chunks (with leaves)
4 small carrots
½ white turnip

1 large onion, cut into chunks
2 sprigs fresh parsley
Salt and pepper to taste

Dumplings:
2 eggs
2 tablespoons cooking oil

½ cup cracker meal
½ teaspoon salt

Remove the skin from the body of the bird, but leave the skin on the legs. Wash the bird in warm salty water. Place the bird in a large pot and add enough cold water to cover. Bring the water to a boil. If scum forms (caused by fat in bird), remove it with a large spoon. Cover the pot, reduce the heat, and gently simmer for 1 hour. Add the celery, carrots, turnip, onion, and parsley. Add salt and pepper to taste.

Bring the liquid to a boil again, once more removing any scum that forms. Cover the pot, reduce the heat, and simmer for 1½ hours longer, or until the bird is very tender.

Meanwhile, make the dumplings. In a mixing bowl, beat the eggs with the oil. Stir in the cracker meal mixed with the salt. Add 2 tablespoons water. Mix all the ingredients together. Cover the bowl and place it in the refrigerator for 1 hour. After chilling the dough, wet your hands with water and form dough lightly into small balls. Approximately 15 minutes before the bird is done, bring the stewing liquid in the pot with the bird back to a boil. Drop the dumplings into the boiling liquid, cover the pot, and reduce heat immediately to a simmer. Do not lift the lid while the dumplings are cooking. They can be tested for doneness after 12 minutes by inserting a toothpick into one of the dumplings. If the toothpick comes out clean, the dumplings are done.

Serves 4.

Saged Sesame Sage Hen

1 breast of sage hen, cleaned and skinned	Salt, pepper, and garlic powder
2 eggs	½ cup sesame seeds
Milk	1½ teaspoons sage
Flour	4 tablespoons butter

Bone the hen breasts and slice them into pieces ¼ inch thick. Lightly beat the eggs and add a little milk. Dip the bird pieces in the egg mixture, then dredge them in flour seasoned with salt, pepper, and garlic powder. Redip the floured bird pieces into the beaten egg, then dredge in a mixture of sesame seeds and sage.

Melt the butter in a large skillet over medium heat. Brown the bird pieces until the crust becomes crisp and golden (about 3 to 5 minutes per side). Pour in ½ cup water and quickly cover. Lower the heat and simmer for about 20 minutes. Remove the cover and continue cooking for another 2 minutes.

Serves 2 to 3.

Roast Sage Hen with Bread Stuffing

1 sage hen, cleaned
Salt, pepper, and garlic
  powder

3 tablespoons melted
  butter

Bread Stuffing:
½ cup butter
½ cup coarsely diced
  onion
½ cup coarsely diced
  celery
½ raw carrot

½ teaspoon salt
¼ teaspoon each of
  pepper and garlic
  powder
1 cup dried bread cubes

Wipe the bird inside and out with a damp paper towel. Sprinkle salt, pepper, and garlic powder over the bird and inside the cavity. Soak a length of cheesecloth (large enough to cover bird) in melted butter and set it aside until the bird is stuffed.

To prepare the stuffing: Melt the butter in a skillet and add the onion and celery. Lightly grate the carrot directly over the skillet and mix it with the onion and celery. Add the salt, pepper, and garlic powder; stir. Sauté the vegetables until soft, push them to the side of the skillet, and add the dried bread cubes. (Take stale bread or sliced white bread cut into ½-inch cubes, put them in a single layer on a cookie sheet, and heat in a moderate oven until the cubes are dried out.) Mix the bread cubes in the melted butter, constantly stirring the cubes until they are all well coated and have absorbed all the butter. If the cubes look dry, add a little more butter.

Allow the bread-cube–vegetable mixture to cool, then spoon it loosely into the cavity of the bird, and skewer closed.

Place the butter-soaked cheesecloth over the bird in a roasting pan. Roast, breast up, in a 350-degree oven for about 1¼ hours, or until the bird is tender, basting frequently with the pan drippings.

Serves 2 to 3.

Broiled Quail

4 quail, cleaned
Salt and pepper
¼ cup melted butter

Split each quail in half and place it cut-side down on a well-buttered broiler rack. Season with salt and pepper. Brush with melted butter. Broil for 15 to 20 minutes, or until browned. Brush frequently with melted butter. Serve on toast.

Serves 2.

Tater Fried Quail

8 quail, cleaned and
  skinned
2 eggs
Salt and pepper
½ teaspoon garlic
  powder

2 cups dehydrated potato
  flakes
1 tablespoon dried
  parsley flakes
4 tablespoons butter

Lightly beat the eggs and add the salt, pepper, and garlic powder. Dip the quail into the egg mixture, then roll it in the potato flakes mixed with dried parsley. Dip it again into the eggs; roll it once more in potato flakes. The birds should now have a heavy crust. Melt the butter in a skillet and brown the quail on all sides. Add ½ cup water to the skillet; cover and let the quail steam for about 8 minutes. Remove the cover and cook for another 2 minutes to crisp up the crust.

Serves 4.

Rice-Stuffed Quail

10 quail, cleaned
1 box prepared wild rice
  or 2 cups brown rice

½ cup red wine
3 tablespoons butter,
  melted

Prepare the rice according to the package directions. Lightly stuff the rice into the quail. Pour about 1 teaspoon wine into each bird. Place the birds in a greased casserole. Add the remaining rice around and on top of the birds. Baste with melted butter. Pour the remainder of the wine over the quail and rice. Cover and bake for 1 hour at 350 degrees.

Serves 4 to 5.

Quail with All-Game Dressing

4 quail, cleaned
Salt and pepper
½ cup melted butter

All-Game Dressing:
1 cup bread crumbs
⅓ cup finely chopped
  celery
⅓ cup onion, finely
  chopped
¼ teaspoon poultry
  seasoning

¼ teaspoon dried savory
⅛ teaspoon powdered
  rosemary
¼ cup beef broth
½ beaten egg

First prepare the stuffing by combining all the ingredients. Lightly spoon stuffing into the cavity of each bird. Place the birds breast up in a buttered baking dish or casserole. Brush with melted butter and sprinkle with salt and pepper. Roast, uncovered, in a preheated 425-degree oven for about 14 minutes, basting often with the melted butter.

Serves 2.

There is something exotic about a flaming entrée. This is a simple recipe to follow. The flambé adds the enchantment.

Quail Flambé

10 quail, cleaned and
   skinned
Salt and pepper
3/4 cup butter
1 teaspoon dry basil

1/2 cup plus 3 tablespoons
   good brandy
4 1/2-ounce can chopped
   black olives

Sprinkle the quail with salt and pepper. Melt the butter in a large frypan over low heat. Stir in the basil. Add the birds and sauté, stirring constantly, for about 5 minutes. Add ½ cup brandy and the olives and stir thoroughly. Cover and reduce the heat. Simmer for 20 to 25 minutes, basting frequently. If more liquid is necessary, add a little brandy.

To flame: Bring the quail to the table in the pan. Uncover and add 3 tablespoons of brandy to the pan. Flame with a long taper.

Serves 4 to 5.

Quail Paprika

6 quail, cleaned
1 teaspoon salt
¼ teaspoon pepper
3 tablespoons flour
½ cup butter

2 10¾-ounce cans cream
of mushroom soup
3 tablespoons paprika
¾ cup sour cream

Rub the quail inside and out with salt and pepper. Tie the legs close to the body. Sprinkle with 2 tablespoons of the flour. Brown the quail in butter for 6 minutes. Place the birds in a casserole.

In a mixing bowl combine the soup, 1 cup water, and paprika, and stir until well blended. Pour the sauce over the quail. Bake, covered, in a moderate oven (350 degrees) for 25 minutes, or until tender. Remove the quail to a warm platter. Stir the remaining flour into the pan juices. Add the sour cream, mix, and heat but do not allow the sauce to come to a boil. Season to taste. Pour the sauce over the quail.

Serves 2 to 3.

*Your pantry shelves hold numerous everyday items that
can suddenly become gourmet ingredients. For example, in
this recipe a breakfast cereal, once crushed, becomes a terrific
crust.*

Quail en Chex

4 quail, cleaned
¾ cup crushed Corn
  Chex (breakfast cereal)
3 tablespoons flour
1 teaspoon salt
¼ teaspoon pepper

⅛ teaspoon cayenne
  pepper
1 egg
½ cup milk
½ cup butter

Wash the quail and pat dry. Tie the legs close to the
body. Combine the Chex crumbs, flour, salt, pepper, and
cayenne pepper. Beat together the egg and milk. Dip
the quail in the milk mixture; roll them in the crumb
mixture. Brown the quail well in butter. Cover and cook
over low heat for 30 minutes, or until tender.

Serves 2.

Quail in Creamed Celery

8 quail, cleaned and
  skinned
10¾-ounce can
  condensed cream of
  celery soup
1 cup sour cream
1 cup chicken broth (or
  bouillon)
½ cup sherry
1 teaspoon paprika

½ teaspoon dry mustard
4 tablespoons fresh
  parsley, coarsely
  chopped
4 large celery stalks,
  coarsely diced
4 tablespoons butter
Salt, pepper, and garlic
  powder

The sauce should be made first: Blend the cream of celery soup, sour cream, chicken broth, sherry, paprika, dry mustard, and chopped parsley (reserve a little parsley for garnish). Set the soup mixture aside. Melt the butter in a large skillet. Place the quail and celery in the butter; add salt, pepper, and garlic powder to taste. Sauté the birds until they are golden-brown, approximately 3 minutes on each side. Add the soup mixture directly to the skillet, stir, cover. Lower the heat and simmer for 30 minutes.

Serves 4.

Skillet Quail

8 quail, cleaned
4 tablespoons butter
1 cup shredded carrot
1/2 cup sliced green
    onions (scallions)
1/4 cup fresh snipped
    parsley

1 cup long-grain rice
3 cups chicken broth
1/2 teaspoon salt
Dash of pepper
2 strips bacon, cut up

Brown the whole birds in the butter, then remove them and set aside. In the same skillet cook the carrots, onions, and parsley until tender, stirring often. Add the rice and mix thoroughly. Add the chicken broth, salt, and pepper. Place the birds on top of the mixture. Sprinkle with additional salt and pepper. Place some bacon on top of each bird. Cover and cook for 30 minutes, or until tender. Remove the bacon and serve.

Serves 4.

Quail in Cassis

10 quail, cleaned and
 skinned

Marinade:
1½ cups Cassis
 (black-currant liqueur)

⅓ cup cooking oil
Salt and pepper

Cassis Sauce:
1 cup marinade (reserved
 from above)
½ cup Cassis liqueur
1 tablespoon black cherry
 jam

1 cup chicken broth (or
 bouillon)
½ cup seedless white
 raisins
3 tablespoons flour

Combine the marinade ingredients. Pour the marinade into a large shallow pan and add the quail. Cover and refrigerate for 4 hours, turning the birds once. After the quail are marinated, remove them from the pan; reserve 1 cup of the marinade for the sauce. Boil 1 cup water and pour it over the raisins; cover and let them steep for 5 minutes.

In the meantime, make the sauce by combining the marinade, liqueur, jam, and chicken broth. Heat slowly at low temperature; gradually add flour to thicken the sauce, stirring constantly. Drain the raisins and add them to the sauce. Arrange the quail in a single layer, breast up, in a baking dish. Pour the sauce on top. Cover and bake at 350 degrees for 30 minutes.

Serves 4 to 5.

Indonesian Quail

8 quail, cleaned and
   skinned
16 strips bacon
2 tablespoons flour

Salt and pepper
1 cup peanut butter
1 teaspoon curry powder

Pat the birds dry with a paper towel, then set them aside. Cook the bacon until well done. Drain the bacon on a paper towel, crumble bacon, and set it aside. Dredge the birds lightly in the flour. Sprinkle with salt and pepper. Thickly coat each bird with peanut butter that has been mixed with curry powder, then roll it in the crumbled bacon. Place the quail on a cookie sheet and bake at 375 degrees for 25 minutes.

Serves 4.

Quail in Nest

6 quail, cleaned
1 loaf unsliced dry bread
Butter
Salt and pepper

½ cup chicken broth
3 ounces brandy
1 cup white grapes

Cut unsliced bread into 6 ovals, each 2 inches thick, or slightly larger than a quail. Remove an oval-shaped area from the center of the bread slices to nest each bird. Toast the bread (*croustade*) gently in a slow oven. Butter the sides of the nest cavities.

Brown the quail quickly in butter; add salt and pepper to taste. Add the broth to the pan. Cover, reduce the heat, and simmer for 10 minutes. Add the brandy and white grapes. Cover and simmer for another 5 to 8 minutes. Serve each quail in a *croustade* nest and pass the sauce in a separate dish.

Serves 2 to 3.

Chianti Doves

10 doves, cleaned and
    breasted out (*see* page 16)
2 packages dry spaghetti-
    sauce mix (each about
    1⅓ ounces)

Butter
1 cup chicken broth
1 cup Chianti wine

Pour 2 packages of spaghetti-sauce mix into a plastic bag. Shake the doves in the mix. Brown the birds lightly in butter in a saucepan. Add the chicken broth and wine. Cover, simmer over low heat until tender (about 20 minutes).

Serves 3 to 4.

Dove Casserole

3–4 doves per person
Salt, pepper, oregano, and
    garlic powder
Cooking oil

Packaged cornbread
    dressing
½ cup applesauce per
    serving

After the doves are cleaned, seasoned, and browned in the cooking oil, remove them from the skillet. Prepare a moist cornbread dressing according to the package directions, except substitute applesauce for the water. Spread some of the dressing on the bottom of a greased casserole. Place the birds on top with extra dressing around and over them. Cover with aluminum foil and bake at 300 degrees for 45 minutes.

Most men enjoy the hot, spicy seasonings of Mexican and Spanish dishes. Since this is their game, how about:

La Paloma con Chiles por Dos
(CHICKEN/DOVES WITH CHILES FOR TWO)

8 doves
Salt and pepper
2 tablespoons olive oil
1 large onion, chopped
2 green chile peppers, chopped
1 clove garlic, chopped

Dash of Worcestershire sauce
8-ounce can tomato sauce with onions
1 teaspoon parsley, chopped
¼ teaspoon oregano

Clean the doves thoroughly and sprinkle them with salt and pepper. In a skillet, brown the doves in the oil. Add the onion, green chile peppers, garlic, and a dash of Worcestershire sauce. Stir constantly for 2 minutes. Add the remaining ingredients and enough water to cover the birds. Place lid on skillet and let birds simmer for 1½ hours. Serve with rice.

This makes the meat so tender that it will gently fall away from the bones. *Arriba!*

Serves 2 to 3.

Far Eastern Dove

12 doves, cleaned
3 slices cooked ham (sandwich-style meat)
½ cup pitted green olives

4 tablespoons butter
3 tablespoons powdered ginger
1 cup red wine

Cut up the cooked ham into bite-size pieces and slice the olives; put them aside. In a large skillet, lightly sauté the doves in the butter. Generously sprinkle each bird with ginger and pour in the wine. Add the ham and olives. Cover and simmer for 30 minutes.

Serves 4.

Marinated Dove

8 doves, cleaned and
  breasted out (*see* page 16)
1 apple, peeled, cored,
  and cut into 8 pieces

8 strips bacon
½ cup red wine

Soy-Ginger Marinade:
½ cup soy sauce
½ teaspoon garlic
  powder

½ teaspoon powdered
  ginger
1 cup red wine

Combine all the marinade ingredients in a bowl. Add the doves, then cover and refrigerate overnight. Prior to cooking, remove the doves from the marinade and discard the marinade. Place a piece of apple inside each breast. Fold breast over apple. Wrap a strip of bacon tightly around the breast and apple and secure with a toothpick. Place the doves in a casserole and add the wine. Bake at 350 degrees for 45 minutes, or until tender, basting occasionally with the pan juices. Remove the toothpicks before serving.

Serves 2 to 3.

Dove Gumbo

12 – 18 dove breasts
Cooking oil
1 cup fresh or canned
  okra, sliced
1 large green pepper,
  sliced
1 small red pepper, sliced
1 cup chopped celery
¼ cup chopped onion
¼ cup shredded parsley

2 cans condensed chicken
  with rice soup
1 chicken bouillon cube
¼ cup vermouth
  (optional)
2 cups peeled tomatoes
  (canned)
16-ounce can corn
1 – 2 teaspoons filé
  powder

Carefully fillet the dove breasts from the bone. Allow three breasts (six fillets) per hungry appetite. Sauté the fillets in oil with the okra, peppers, celery, onion, and parsley for approximately 5 minutes.

In a large kettle, mix the soup with an equal amount of water, add bouillon cube and vermouth, and bring to a full boil. Add the dove-vegetable mixture, tomatoes, and corn. Cover and simmer until tender (about 30 minutes).

Moisten filé powder with water and add to kettle. Stir. Simmer, uncovered, for another 5 minutes.

Serves 6.

Dove breasts in paper is a popular French delicacy.

Doves en Papillotes
(HORS D'OEUVRES)

4 doves, breasted and
  boned (makes 8 fillets)
Salt and pepper
8 strips bacon, chopped
2 tablespoons butter
4 tablespoons cooking oil

½ cup fresh mushrooms,
  chopped
4 – 5 sprigs parsley,
  chopped
2 shallots, chopped

Season the dove breasts with salt and pepper. Cook the bacon in a skillet until done, then remove the pieces with a slotted spoon. Add the butter and oil to the skillet with the bacon drippings. Sauté the mushrooms and dove breasts until the breasts are golden. Remove the skillet from the heat and add the parsley, shallots, and bacon pieces. Place each breast on a large square of oiled paper or foil. Spoon some pan mixture over each breast. Turn the ends of paper to seal. Bake for 30 minutes in a 350-degree oven. Serve the doves in their paper wrap. An ideal party appetizer.

Doves with Grapes and Wine

12 doves, cleaned
2 onions, sliced ¼ inch
   thick
2 cups seedless grapes
   (retain juice if you are
   using canned grapes
   and add to the recipe
   liquid)

Salt and pepper
3 tablespoons butter
½ cup melted butter
½ cup dry white wine
1 cup chicken broth

Stuff each dove with onion slices and a few grapes. Close the openings with fine skewers and season the outside with salt and pepper. Brown the birds in the 3 tablespoons of butter. Combine the melted butter, wine, and broth to make a basting liquid. Brush the outside of the birds with this baste. Place the birds in a baking dish and roast in 350-degree oven for 45 minutes, basting frequently.

Serves 4.

Happy Hour Hawaiian Doves
(HORS D'OEUVRES)

Dove breasts (quantity
depends on number of
guests)
Butter
1 medium jar apricot-
pineapple preserves

1 medium bottle teriyaki
sauce (or homemade —
see page 27)
1 cup sesame seeds

Bone the dove breasts and sauté them lightly in butter. On a large working surface, lay out individual squares of aluminum foil (about 3 inches). Place one breast on each square and top with 1 teaspoon of apricot-pineapple preserves and 1 tablespoon of teriyaki sauce. Seal the foil tightly and bake at 400 degrees for 20 minutes.

When serving, place the foil packages on a hot platter to keep warm. Pour sesame seeds into a small serving bowl. Encourage your guests to open each package and then roll one dove at a time in the sesame seeds. Chopsticks, bamboo skewers, or toothpicks will be helpful when eating.

Extra-Special Doves with Grapes and Wine

10 doves, cleaned and
wet from washing
3 – 4 strips bacon
Flour
Salt and pepper
1 cup chicken consommé
1 cup Sauterne wine (or
for another flavor, try
claret)

1 stalk celery
3 carrots, thinly sliced
½ cup sliced mushrooms,
sautéed
2 cups seedless grapes (if
canned grapes, retain
juice and add to recipe
liquid)
½ cup orange juice

Fry the bacon until it is half cooked, then remove the bacon and save the drippings. Dredge the doves in flour seasoned with salt and pepper. Sauté the birds in the bacon drippings. Next arrange the doves in a baking dish and place a small piece of bacon across each upturned breast. Add the consommé, wine, celery stalk, and carrots. Cover and bake at 325 degrees for 20 minutes. Then add the grapes and mushrooms. Cover and cook for another 15 minutes. Add the orange juice and cover once again for the final 15 minutes of cooking. Remove and discard the celery.

Serves 3 to 4.

For an appetizer, luncheon, or brunch.

Mushrooms Stuffed with Dove

This recipe makes 2 stuffed mushrooms; increase as desired.

1 dove breast
2 tablespoons butter
Salt, pepper, and garlic
   powder to taste
1 tablespoon diced fresh
   onion
2 extra-large fresh

mushrooms
2 teaspoons grated
   Parmesan cheese
1 teaspoon dry sherry
Dash of Worcestershire
   sauce

Bone the dove breast (which will give you two fillets). Melt 1 tablespoon of the butter in a frypan; add the fillets, salt, pepper, garlic powder, and onion. Sauté for 8 to 10 minutes, turning constantly to avoid sticking. Remove the fillets from the pan; set them aside. Wash the fresh mushrooms, remove the stems, and set them aside. Sauté the caps, head down, in 1 tablespoon butter for 2 to 3 minutes, then set them aside. On a cutting board, trim off the hard end of the mushroom stems and discard. Finely chop the remainder of the stems and the sautéed fillets. Combine the onion and pan drippings in a mixing bowl. Add the Parmesan cheese, sherry, and Worcestershire sauce. If the mixture seems dry, moisten with more wine or melted butter.

Stuff the mushroom caps with the mixture and place, stuffing-side up, in an oiled baking dish. Bake at 425 degrees for 10 minutes. Average serving: 2 to 3 caps per person for brunch or luncheon. This is also an ideal stuffing for baked green peppers or broiled tomatoes.

Steamed Pigeon

12 pigeons, cleaned
4 stalks celery, coarsely chopped
3 medium onions, sliced ¼ inch thick

2 whole garlic cloves
¼ cup olive oil
½ cup white wine (you may substitute chicken broth)

Sauté the celery, onions, and garlic in the olive oil. Remove the garlic and add the pigeons. Lightly brown the birds (it should take about 4 minutes). Pour in the wine or other liquid. Cover and steam for 25 minutes, or until the pigeons are tender.

Serves 4.

Pigeon in Fruited Yogurt

12 pigeons, breasted out
  (*see* page 16)
Salt and pepper
8-ounce container

blueberry yogurt
1 ½ cups shredded
  coconut

Sprinkle salt and pepper on the pigeons. Roll the pigeons in the yogurt, coating them thickly, then roll them in the coconut, completely covering the birds. The birds should resemble snowballs. Bake them on a greased cookie sheet at 400 degrees for about 15 to 18 minutes, taking care so that coconut does not get too dark.

For variation, try spiced apple, Concord grape, or boysenberry yogurt.

Serves 4.

Due to its small size, the pigeon breast is ideally suited to finger foods.

Pigeon Rumaki
(HORS D'OEUVRES OR APPETIZER)

10 pigeon breasts
7 water chestnuts, sliced
  in thirds

Salt and pepper
10 strips bacon, cut in
  half

Bone out the pigeon breasts, which will give you two fillets per breast. Salt and pepper each breast, placing a slice of water chestnut in the center. Fold the ends of the breast over the water chestnut. Wrap ½ slice of bacon around each breast and secure with a toothpick. Place the breasts in a baking pan. Broil for 3 minutes, turn the breasts over, and broil for 3 minutes more. Increase the recipe according to number of Rumakis desired.

Makes 20 Rumakis.

Simple Pigeon Pastries
(HORS D'OEUVRES, APPETIZER, OR LUNCHEON)

Basic ingredients (for 2 pastries):

1 pigeon breast
1 tablespoon butter
Salt and pepper

Packaged refrigerator
buttermilk biscuits

Filling Variations:

A. 2 tablespoons
    liverwurst
    2 teaspoons prepared
    mustard
B. 1 tablespoon pickle
    relish
    2 tablespoons grated
    Cheddar cheese

C. 2 tablespoons apple
    butter
    2 tablespoons whole
    cranberry sauce

Bone out the pigeon breast, which will give you two fillets. Sauté the fillets in butter with salt and pepper, turning them so that they do not stick to the pan (cook for about 3 minutes on each side). Roll out the packaged biscuits (one biscuit per pastry) on waxed paper or a lightly floured flat surface, to ⅛ inch thickness, oval shaped.

Spread the desired filling in layers on the dough, making sure the entire surface is evenly covered. Place one fillet on the bottom half of the dough, fold over the top half, and seal the edges closed with a fork. Gently prick holes on the top. Repeat the procedure for the second pastry. Bake on a greased cookie sheet at 475 degrees for 10 minutes, or until the biscuits are golden. Increase the recipe for the desired number of pastries.

Makes 2.

Savory Pigeon Pastry
(HORS D'OEUVRES, APPETIZER, OR LUNCHEON)

1 pigeon breast
1 ½ tablespoons butter
2 tablespoons diced
  celery
2 tablespoons diced fresh
  onion
Salt, pepper, and garlic
  powder to taste

½ teaspoon
  Worcestershire sauce
1 teaspoon mayonnaise
Packaged refrigerator
  buttermilk biscuits

Bone out the pigeon breast, which will give you two fillets. Sauté the fillets in butter with the celery, onion, salt, pepper, and garlic powder for about 10 minutes. Stir constantly so that the fillets do not stick to the pan. Set aside the onion, celery, and pan drippings in a mixing bowl. Place the cooked fillets on a cutting board, chop coarsely, and add to the ingredients in the mixing bowl. Sprinkle with Worcestershire sauce and add the mayonnaise.

On waxed paper or a lightly floured flat surface, roll out 2 biscuits into oval shapes, each approximately ⅛ inch thick. Place half of the pigeon mixture on the lower half of one of the biscuits. Fold over the top half and seal the edges closed by pressing with a fork. Gently prick holes on the top. Repeat the procedure for the second pastry. Place the pastries on a greased baking sheet and bake at 475 degrees for 10 minutes, or until the biscuits are golden. Increase the recipe according to the number of pastries desired.

Makes 2 medium-size pastries.

WATERFOWL

The natural habitat of wild ducks and geese is water. Therefore, their diet generally features fish, shellfish, mollusks, and aquatic plants. These eating habits result in the waterfowl having a gamy taste, which can be reduced by utilizing one of our special handling tips.

Special Handling Tips for Wild Ducks and Geese

1. For wild geese, advise your hunter to bleed them in the field. This will reduce their gaminess considerably.

2. Parboil waterfowl for 15 to 20 minutes, depending on their quantity and size, with your choice of:
   a. herbs
   b. any combination of carrot, onion, celery, apple pieces, juniper berries, or parsley placed in the cavity
   c. ½ cup white wine added to the water with sliced garlic cloves or ¼ cup lemon juice or ¼ cup vinegar with garlic.

3. Wash the birds thoroughly inside and out under cold running water. Refrigerate overnight in salted water to cover. Rinse in clear water and dry thoroughly before cooking.

4. Rub the cleaned bird inside and out with a handful of raw cranberries, crushing them against the flesh. Refrigerate overnight with berries. Wash well the next day.

5. Brush the bird inside and out with sherry (or Burgundy). Refrigerate for 6 hours, brushing the bird occasionally with sherry.

6. Take a sharp knife and make a small slit in the breast skin, pull the skin back, and cut out the fat.

7. When roasting a bird that is not going to be stuffed, place a piece of peeled lemon, a small peeled onion, or some apple slices into the cavity; remove them before serving the cooked bird.

8. Since the gamy taste is most pronounced in the fat of wild duck and goose, we reduce the gaminess by reducing the fat via the suggested methods. However, in order to keep wild duck and goose from becoming too dry while roasting, we suggest covering the birds with slices of salt pork, bacon, or cheesecloth soaked in oil or melted butter.

9. To tenderize large birds while roasting, add 1 cup of boiling water to the pan and cover tightly for the last hour of cooking. Smaller birds will require less steaming time.

Traditional Orange Duck Made Easy

1 duck, cleaned and
  parboiled
½ cup orange marmalade
1 large orange (not
  peeled)
½ cup Grand Marnier or

Cointreau (or other
  orange liqueur)
Toasted almond slivers or
  candied maraschino
  cherries (optional
  garnish)

Split the duck in half lengthwise and place it in a baking pan. Generously spoon some marmalade on top. Slice the orange into ¼-inch rings and place them around the duck. Add ¼ cup of the liqueur. Bake, uncovered, in a 375-degree oven for 45 minutes, or until tender. About every 15 minutes, baste with marmalade and sprinkle with liqueur. When serving, garnish with the orange slices and some almond slivers or candied maraschino cherries, if you wish. This makes a romantic candlelight dinner for 2.

VARIATION: Substitute canned crushed pineapple for the orange and ¼ cup bourbon and ¼ cup sherry for the orange liqueur.

Duck with Bing Cherries

4 ducks, approximately 3
  pounds each

4 cups of your favorite
  dressing

Bing Cherry Sauce:
2 large cans (1-pound-5-
  ounce size) pitted Bing
  cherries

1 cup red port wine
2 tablespoons cornstarch

Stuff the cleaned birds with your favorite dressing. (Or, for unstuffed ducks, insert a few celery stalks and onion slices in each bird. After roasting, discard these vegetables.)

Roast the ducks, uncovered, in a 375-degree oven

for about 1 hour, or until tender. Split each roasted duck in half lengthwise. Top with hot Bing Cherry Sauce.

To make Bing Cherry Sauce: Drain the cherries and set them aside. Add the wine to the juice and bring to a boil. Mix the cornstarch with a few drops of cold water to make a paste. Add to the liquid to thicken. Reduce heat to a simmer. Add the Bing cherries.

Serves 8.

Roast Mallard with Filbert Stuffing

2 mallards, cleaned
1 ½ teaspoons salt
½ teaspoon pepper

½ cup melted butter
2 tablespoons lemon
 juice

Filbert Stuffing:
½ cup chopped onion
½ cup diced celery with
 leaves
¼ cup butter
2 cups dry bread crumbs
½ cup coarsely chopped
 filberts

¾ cup giblet stock or
 chicken bouillon
½ teaspoon salt
½ teaspoon powdered
 thyme
⅛ teaspoon pepper

Prepare the stuffing first: Cook the onion and celery in the butter until tender, then add to the bread crumbs and nuts in a mixing bowl. Toss lightly and add the stock to moisten. Mix in the seasonings.

Rub the ducks inside and out with salt and pepper. Combine the butter and lemon juice and brush the birds inside and out with the mixture. Spoon the stuffing into the ducks. Truss the birds, wrap them in aluminum foil, and place them in a shallow pan. Bake in a 325-degree oven for 1 ½ hours. Uncover the birds and baste them with the butter mixture. Continue baking for another 30 minutes, or until the birds are brown. Baste every 10 minutes. · *Serves 4.*

Ducks Smothered with Onions and Mushrooms

2 ducks, cleaned and
  parboiled
2 large onions, cut into
  1/4-inch rings
1/2 pound small fresh
  mushrooms, sliced in
  half

3 tablespoons butter
1/2 cup sherry
Salt and pepper
Paprika
10 3/4-ounce can onion
  soup

Sauté the onions and mushrooms in the butter in a large heavy skillet. Pour in 1/4 cup of the sherry. Cover and simmer for 10 minutes. Split the ducks in half lengthwise. Salt and pepper the birds and add them to the pan with the sautéed vegetables. Sprinkle generously with paprika. Pour in the onion soup and remaining sherry. Cover again and cook over medium heat for 45 minutes.

Serves 4.

Breast of Duck Stroganoff

5 ducks (breasts only)
1 small onion, diced
1/2 green pepper
4 tablespoons butter
2 6-ounce cans mushroom
  sauce
3-ounce can mushrooms
  (with liquid)

1/2 pint sour cream
1 cup red wine
Dash of Worcestershire
  sauce
1/4 teaspoon each of garlic
  powder, basil, and
  thyme
1/2 teaspoon oregano

Bone the duck breasts and cut them into cubes. Brown the onion, green pepper, and duck together in the butter. Add the mushroom sauce, mushrooms and liquid, sour cream, wine, Worcestershire sauce, and all the spices and herbs. Simmer, covered, for 1 hour.

Serves 4 to 6.

Barbecued Duck in a Beer-Orange Marinade

10 ducks, skinned

Beer-Orange Marinade:

6 12-ounce cans beer
2 12-ounce cans frozen
   concentrated orange
   juice, defrosted
1 tablespoon whole
   peppercorns
1 tablespoon minced
   onions

1 teaspoon celery seeds
1/2 teaspoon each of
   paprika, nutmeg, garlic
   powder, and "liquid
   smoke"
1 teaspoon
   Worcestershire sauce

Split each duck in half lengthwise. Combine all the marinade ingredients in a large pot or bowl. Add the ducks and marinate in the refrigerator for 36 hours. Barbecue over hot coals for about 40 minutes, basting constantly with the marinade.

Serves 10 to 15.

Years ago professional hunters would bring the best eating ducks to market in canvas bags. Occasionally, the dealers would misplace these bags once they had removed the game for hanging. To bring an end to this carelessness, the hunters marked in bold letters on their bags, "Return My Canvas Back." And so the best eating ducks came to be known as "canvasbacks." Well, maybe that's the way it went.

Roast Canvasback in Port Wine

2 ducks, cleaned
2 lemons
Salt and pepper
1 teaspoon minced
   shallot (or onion)
1 sprig thyme

Juice of 2 oranges
1/4 teaspoon grated
   orange rind
Pinch of cayenne
1 tablespoon flour
1 cup hot chicken broth

Port Wine Marinade:

2 cups port wine
1 small onion, sliced

3 cloves
1 large bay leaf

Rub the ducks inside and out with the juice of one lemon and sprinkle with salt and pepper. Place the birds in a large bowl or pan. Cover with Port Wine Marinade and refrigerate for 24 hours.

When you are ready to prepare the ducks: Combine in saucepan 1 cup of the strained marinade with the minced shallot, thyme, orange juice, orange rind, and the juice of the second lemon. Add the cayenne and salt. Reduce the sauce by half. Blend the flour with water and add it to the sauce. Stir in the hot chicken broth. Place the ducks on a rack in a roasting pan and brush with the marinade. Bake in a 350-degree oven for 1 hour, basting often with the marinade sauce.

Serves 4.

Rotisseried Duck with Parsley-Orange Glaze

1 mallard, cleaned
⅓ cup butter
1½ cups fresh orange
  juice
½ cup white wine
3 tablespoons sugar
1 teaspoon grated orange
  peel
¾ teaspoon salt
⅛ teaspoon dry mustard
Salt and pepper, a dash
  each

½ large orange, peeled
1 medium onion, cut in
  half
2 tablespoons melted
  butter
¼ teaspoon dried
  rosemary
4 strips salt pork
1 teaspoon cornstarch
2 tablespoons chopped
  parsley

Heat together the butter, orange juice, wine, sugar, orange peel, salt, and mustard until the butter melts. Keep the butter warm while preparing the duck. Season the inside of the mallard with salt and pepper. Stuff the orange and onion into the cavity. Combine the melted butter with the rosemary and pour it into the duck. Cover the breast with the strips of salt pork and fasten with skewers. Arrange the bird on the spit. Cook at a high heat (425 degrees) for 1 hour, or until done. Baste every 15 minutes with the orange glaze. (Or, bake in a 475-degree oven for 35 to 40 minutes. Baste every 10 minutes.)

Split the duck with a very sharp knife or shears and place it on a hot platter. Mix the cornstarch in a little cold water and then stir it into the remaining orange glaze. Heat and stir until the glaze is thickened. Add the parsley. Pour the glaze over the duck. Garnish with the orange slices.

Serves 2.

Honeyed Duck

1 duck, cleaned
2 teaspoons salt
1 teaspoon ground ginger
1 teaspoon ground basil
1/2 teaspoon pepper
3/4 cup honey
1/4 cup butter
3 tablespoons orange
   juice

2 teaspoons lemon juice
1 teaspoon orange peel
1/8 teaspoon dry mustard
1 unpeeled orange, cut
   into 1/2-inch slices
1/2 teaspoon cornstarch

Combine the salt, ginger, basil, and pepper. Rub half of the mixture inside the duck. Heat together the honey, butter, orange juice, lemon juice, orange peel, and mustard, stirring until the butter melts. Rub the inside of the duck with 2 to 3 tablespoons of the mixture.

Stuff the duck with the orange slices. Pour 4 to 5 more tablespoons of the honey mixture into the bird. Truss the duck and rub remaining seasoning mixture over the outside of the duck.

Place the bird on a large piece of heavy-duty aluminum foil. Cover with the remaining honey mixture. Wrap the duck and roast at 325 degrees for 1¾ hours. Unwrap and baste with drippings, then bake for another 20 to 25 minutes, or until brown. Place the duck on a hot platter to keep warm.

Combine the cornstarch with a little cold water and add it to the drippings. Stir and heat to boiling. Serve over the duck.

Serves 2.

Orange Duck Flambé — Mmmm

2 ducks, cleaned and split in half lengthwise	1 orange
	1 lemon
6-ounce can frozen orange juice	2 tablespoons cornstarch
	1 teaspoon thyme
1 cup powdered sugar	1 apple
½ teaspoon each of salt, pepper, and ground ginger	1 medium onion
	4 tablespoons cognac

In a mixing bowl combine the frozen orange juice, 2½ cups water, powdered sugar, salt, pepper, and ginger. Rub the orange and lemon on a grater until you have 1 teaspoon each of rind. Add the grated rind, cornstarch, thyme, and 1 teaspoon juice from the lemon to the mixing bowl. Mix all the ingredients thoroughly and transfer to a saucepan. Stir constantly over medium heat and bring to a boil. The mixture should thicken tremendously. As soon as it reaches the boil, turn off the heat.

Wash the split ducks and pat dry. Tear off four large pieces of heavy-duty foil. Place each duck half on foil, skin-side down. Cut the apple, onion, and the remaining orange and lemon into thin slices. (Don't peel the fruit.) Place the fruit and onion inside the duck cavities. Fill each with as much sauce as it will hold (approximately ½ cup). Wrap each carefully with the foil so as not to spill the liquid. Bake for about 30 minutes in a 425-degree oven; or, place the packages on a medium-hot barbecue grill.

After 30 minutes, remove the duck from the oven. Carefully unwrap each package and pour the fruit and juice back into the saucepan, and place it over low heat to keep the sauce warm. Put the birds on a cookie sheet under the broiler, skin-side up. Brown until the skin is crisp.

To serve, place the birds on a large platter, spoon the sauce on top, and add the cognac and flame.

Serves 4.

A favorite dish of Philippine cooks is Adobo, in which various meats, fowl, or combinations of both are cooked in a spicy soy sauce. We find this Adobo preparation of duck most enjoyable.

Duck Adobo
(PHILIPPINE STYLE)

6 whole duck breasts (on bone)
2 teaspoons vinegar
1/8 teaspoon black pepper
1/2 onion, cut into chunks
3 garlic cloves, mashed
1/4 cup cooking oil
Juice of 1 lemon
1 cup soy sauce

Remove the skin and cut the breasts in half (leave on bone). Cut each half into half again; this will give you twenty-four quarters. Place the duck pieces in a pot. Add water—slightly less than to cover. Bring to a boil and continue boiling until tender. Add the vinegar, pepper, onion, and garlic. Cover the pot and continue cooking over high heat until the liquid is reduced to approximately 1/2 cup. Add the oil and cook over high heat for 5 minutes. Combine the lemon juice and soy sauce and add them to the duck pieces. Continue cooking for 10 minutes. Serve with hot white rice.

Serves 4 to 6.

Duck Oriental

2 ducks, cleaned
3 tablespoons melted
  butter
16-ounce can
  pineapple chunks
  (and juice)

1 green pepper, cut into
  thin strips
1 onion, cut into thin
  rings
1 package frozen
  Chinese pea pods

Oriental Marinade:
1 cup soy sauce
½ cup brown sugar
½ teaspoon ginger

¼ teaspoon garlic
  powder

Remove the duck meat from the bones and cut into bite-size pieces. Combine the ingredients for the Oriental Marinade in a large bowl and marinate the duck pieces for 2 to 3 hours. Remove the duck from the marinade and brush with melted butter. Place the duck in a shallow baking pan and bake for 30 minutes at 350 degrees. Turn the pieces and add the pineapple chunks with juice, green pepper, and onion rings. Continue cooking for 1 hour. During last 15 minutes add the frozen pea pods and cover the pan. Baste occasionally with the juice from the pan.

Serves 4.

Pollo en Jugo de Naranja
(SPANISH BIRD IN ORANGE JUICE)

2 ducks, parboiled
Flour
Oil (preferably Spanish
  olive oil)
1 cup fresh orange juice
1 cup white wine
½ cup raisins

½ cup blanched ground
  almonds
½ cup crushed pineapple
2 tablespoons sugar
¼ teaspoon cinnamon
⅛ teaspoon cloves

Split the ducks in half lengthwise. Dredge them in flour and brown in oil. Place the birds in a shallow glass baking dish. Combine all the other ingredients and pour them over the duck. Bake at 350 degrees for 30 minutes, basting often. Raise the oven temperature to 400 degrees and bake for another 15 minutes.

Serves 2 to 4.

Mallards in Mushroom Sauce

4 mallards, cleaned
Salt and pepper
½ teaspoon paprika
½ cup flour

¼ cup cooking oil
1 apple, quartered
1 orange, quartered
1 onion, quartered

Mushroom Sauce:
10¾-ounce can
  condensed cream of
  mushroom soup
10¾-ounce can beef
  bouillon
½ cup sherry
½ cup chopped

  mushrooms
Dash of Worcestershire
  sauce
1 teaspoon parsley flakes
½ teaspoon salt
¼ teaspoon paprika

Sprinkle the ducks with salt and pepper. Add the paprika to the flour and dredge the birds in the flour mixture, then brown them lightly in cooking oil. Remove the birds from the skillet and stuff each one with apple, orange, and onion pieces. Place the ducks in a baking pan or roaster.

In a separate pan combine all the sauce ingredients, adding 2 soup cans of water. Stir and cook until the sauce is hot, then pour it over the stuffed game in the roaster. Cover and bake at 350 degrees for 1½ hours, or until the ducks are tender, occasionally basting with the sauce.

Serves 6.

Some hunters think mudhen (coot) is unfit to eat because of its strong "fishy" flavor and tough texture. However, with proper handling and marinating, coot can offer some mighty tasty eating.

Mudhen Sweet 'n' Sour

16 mudhen, breasted out
   and boned (32 fillets)
   (*see* page 16)

1 cup chili sauce
1 cup grape jelly

Combine the chili sauce and grape jelly in a large bowl to make a marinade. Wipe off the breasts and place them in the marinade. Cover and refrigerate for 24 to 36 hours. Place the fillets on a grill over hot coals. Barbecue for about 4 minutes on each side, basting often with the marinade.

Serves 6 hungry people.

Pan-Fried Coot Breasts

8 coot breasted out and
boned (16 fillets) (*see*
page 16)
8-ounce can beer
½ teaspoon salt

½ teaspoon pepper
2 eggs lightly beaten
1 cup bread crumbs
⅓ cup cooking oil

Pour the beer into a shallow bowl and add the coot fillets. Cover the bowl, put it in the refrigerator, and allow the fillets to marinate for 24 to 36 hours.

Remove the fillets and discard the marinade. Add the salt and pepper to the beaten eggs, dip the fillets into the egg mixture and then roll in bread crumbs. Pour the cooking oil into a large frypan and heat. Sauté the fillets quickly on each side to brown, then reduce the heat and cook for another 3 minutes on each side.

Serves 2 to 3.

Coot and Spaghetti

8 coot, breasted out and
boned (16 fillets) (*see*
page 16)

Marinara Marinade:
8-ounce can tomato sauce
Dash each of salt, pepper,

garlic powder, and
oregano

Spaghetti Sauce:
2 tablespoons cooking oil
1 onion diced
1 garlic clove minced
¼ teaspoon salt
¼ teaspoon pepper
15-ounce can tomato
sauce
16-ounce can whole
tomatoes
1 teaspoon

Worcestershire sauce
¼ cup grated Parmesan
cheese
½ cup sautéed sliced
mushrooms
½ cup dry red wine
(optional)
12-ounce package
spaghetti

Cut each fillet in half, which will give you thirty-two bite-size pieces. Combine all the marinade ingredients in a bowl, add the coot pieces, and mix through. Cover the bowl and refrigerate for 3 to 6 hours, stirring occasionally.

Remove the pieces and discard the marinade. Put the oil in a saucepan and add the onion, garlic, salt, and pepper. Cook until the onion is soft. Add the coot pieces to the oil and brown lightly on each side, turning often. Remove the coot from the oil. Add the tomato sauce, whole tomatoes, and Worcestershire sauce to the oil, mix, and simmer for 20 minutes.

Return the coot pieces to the oil and tomato sauce mixture and add the Parmesan cheese, mushrooms, and wine. Stir to mix all the ingredients. Continue to simmer for approximately 20 minutes, until the coot pieces are tender. Prepare the spaghetti according to the directions on the package, drain, and place on a large serving platter. Ladle the coot pieces and sauce over the spaghetti. Serve immediately.

Serves 4 to 6.

Curried Coot

8 coot, breasted out and
   boned (16 fillets) (*see*
   page 16)

Curry Marinade:
1 cup chicken broth or
   bouillon
½ teaspoon nutmeg

1 teaspoon curry powder
¼ teaspoon ginger
   powder

Curry Sauce:
¼ cup flour
¼ teaspoon pepper
¼ teaspoon paprika
4 tablespoons butter
1 onion, diced

¼ teaspoon salt
1 tablespoon curry
   powder
1 cup chicken broth or
   bouillon

Cut each fillet in half, which will give you thirty-two pieces. Combine all the marinade ingredients in a bowl and add the coot. Cover the bowl and marinate in the refrigerator for 12 to 24 hours.

Remove the coot and discard the marinade. Combine the flour, pepper, and paprika in a paper bag. Add the coot pieces and shake until well coated with the flour mixture, then remove them from the bag. Melt the butter in a large frypan, sauté the coot lightly on each side, and remove it from the pan. In the same frypan, sauté the onion until soft. Add the salt, curry powder, and chicken broth. If the liquid is thin, blend in ½ tablespoon of the flour mixture from the paper bag to thicken. Return the coot to the pan and lower the heat. Simmer, uncovered, for approximately 25 minutes, or until the coot feels tender when tested with a fork.

Serve with hot white rice and such curry condiments as chutney, raisins, chopped nuts, and tangerine segments.

Serves 4 to 5.

Wild goose is as different from domestic goose as flour is from flower. The trick in preparing domestic goose is to release as much of the fattiness as possible. With wild goose, we must add fat to the bird by barding or basting. The meat of wild goose is dark red, similar to rare beef, and the flavor is quite strong.

Hunter's Roast Young Goose

1 wild goose, cleaned
Salt and pepper
½ cup melted butter

Apricot Stuffing:

2 cups dried apricots
(steeped in hot water)

2 cups bread cubes
2 tablespoons sugar

Fruit Glaze:

1 cup orange juice
½ cup currant jelly

3 tablespoons apricot
brandy

Place the goose in a large pot with cold water to cover and boil for 15 minutes. Remove the goose and dry it thoroughly with paper towels.

Season the goose inside and out with salt and pepper. Stuff it with a combination of dried apricots, bread cubes, sugar, and enough water to moisten.

Put goose in roasting pan with melted butter. Roast the goose at 350 degrees for 18 to 20 minutes per pound, basting frequently with the remaining melted butter. In a saucepan, combine the orange juice, currant jelly, and brandy. Pour the sauce over the goose 20 minutes before serving; continue basting. When serving, pour the remaining sauce into a gravy bowl.

Serves 6.

Ambrosia Roast Goose

1 wild goose, 5 to 6
  pounds, cleaned
1 lemon, cut into
  quarters
Salt and pepper

¼ cup melted bacon fat
4 thick strips bacon
½ cup apple jelly
⅔ cup dry vermouth
½ teaspoon nutmeg

Fruit and Nut Stuffing:

3 Golden Delicious
  apples
2 tablespoons lemon
  juice
1 cup white raisins
  (steeped in hot water)

1 cup chopped walnuts
1 cup cooked white rice
1 teaspoon cinnamon
¼ teaspoon nutmeg
¼ cup brown sugar
¼ cup vermouth

Rub the goose inside and out with the cut lemon and sprinkle with salt and pepper. Set aside.

Core and pare the apples, cut them into chunks, and sprinkle with lemon juice. Combine with the raisins, walnuts, rice, cinnamon, nutmeg, brown sugar, and vermouth. Spoon the stuffing loosely into the goose cavity and skewer closed. Cover the goose with cheesecloth soaked in melted bacon fat, then place bacon strips over cheesecloth. Put goose, breast up, on a rack in a roasting pan. Roast at 325 degrees, basting frequently.

To make the baste: In a saucepan over low heat, mix the apple jelly with the vermouth and nutmeg, stirring until the jelly liquefies. Add the pan drippings and stir.

Roast the bird for approximately 25 minutes per pound until done. If the age of the bird is unknown, tenderize it by pouring 1 cup water into the roasting pan and keeping it covered during the last hour of roasting.

Serves 6 to 8.

According to many bird hunters, the Canadian honker is the prized catch. Here's a regal recipe for this king of birds.

Savory Goose

1 Canadian honker, about
  6 pounds, cleaned
2 cloves garlic

Salt and pepper
¼ cup melted bacon fat
4 thick strips bacon

Savory Stuffing:
2 raw carrots, cut into
  large rounds
4 tablespoons butter
2 cups coarsely diced
  celery
1 large onion, coarsely

    diced
Salt, pepper, paprika, and
  garlic powder
2 cups bread crumbs
4½-ounce can chopped
  black olives

Baste:
1 cup dry red wine
Pan drippings
1 teaspoon basil

Rub the goose inside and out with the garlic. Sprinkle with salt and pepper and set aside.

To make Savory Stuffing: Parboil the carrots until they are almost soft (about 10 minutes). Melt the butter in a skillet, add the celery and onion, and season to taste with salt, pepper, paprika, and garlic powder. Sauté until the celery and onion are soft and then remove the skillet from the heat. Add the bread crumbs, olives, and carrots and mix through. Spoon the stuffing loosely into the goose cavity and skewer closed.

Soak some cheesecloth in melted bacon fat and cover the goose with the cheesecloth. Put the goose, breast up, on a rack in a roasting pan, and place bacon strips over cheesecloth. Roast at 325 degrees for approximately 25 minutes per pound until the bird is done, frequently basting with the red wine combined with the pan drippings and basil. To ensure the tenderness of the bird, pour 1 cup water into the roasting pan and cover during the last hour of cooking.

Serves 6.

For leftover roast goose.

Goose Shepherd's Pie

Goose Mixture:

1 cup leftover roast goose, diced
2 tablespoons cooking oil
Salt and pepper
¼ teaspoon garlic powder

½ onion, diced
Dash of Worcestershire sauce
15-ounce can tomato sauce

Potato Topping:

2 raw potatoes
2 tablespoons butter
⅓ cup milk

1 teaspoon grated
Parmesan cheese
Salt and pepper

To make the Potato Topping: Peel the potatoes, cut them into chunks, put them into a saucepan, and cover with salted water; boil while preparing the Goose Mixture.

Put the oil in a skillet and sauté the onion until soft. Add the diced goose, salt, pepper, garlic powder, and Worcestershire sauce. Stir mixture completely. Add tomato sauce, stir again. Simmer for 3 minutes, then set aside.

When the potatoes are fully cooked, drain off the water. Mash the potatoes until there are no lumps. Add the butter, milk, Parmesan cheese, salt, and pepper, and whip until fluffy. Spread the Goose Mixture evenly in the bottom of the casserole; top with the whipped potatoes. Bake, uncovered, at 350 degrees for 15 minutes.

Serves 4.

Stuffed Goose with Plum Sauce

1 large goose, cleaned
Salt and pepper

1 lemon
4 strips bacon

Chestnut Dressing:
½ cup butter
Goose giblets, chopped,
 or substitute ¼ pound
 chicken giblets
1 cup chopped onions
1 cup chopped celery
1 garlic clove, minced
½ cup chopped parsley
2 cups cooked wild rice
3 cups chestnuts, boiled
 and chopped (fresh
 chestnuts are the best
 although you may

substitute canned)
2 cups apples, peeled,
 cored, and chopped
½ cup seedless raisins,
 soaked in ½ cup Cassis
 liqueur (black-currant
 liqueur)
1 cup brandy (or white
 wine)
1 teaspoon poultry
 seasoning
1 teaspoon cinnamon

Plum Sauce:
1 cup port wine
⅓ cup goose drippings
30-ounce can pitted
 purple plums, drained

½ teaspoon cinnamon
Dash of cayenne
1 tablespoon cornstarch

Melt the butter in a deep skillet. Sauté the chopped giblets with the onions, celery, garlic, and parsley. Add the cooked rice and chestnuts and mix well. Add the fruits and spirits (wines and liqueurs) and season with poultry seasoning and cinnamon. Sprinkle generously with additional Cassis.

Rub the goose inside and out with salt, pepper, and the juice from 1 lemon. Before roasting, fill with the stuffing. Spoon about 1 cup stuffing into the neck cavity and secure it with poultry pins or skewers. Spoon the remaining stuffing into the body cavity. Bake any leftover stuffing in a one-quart casserole during the last 45 minutes of roasting.

Lace the cavity closed with twine or secure with skewers. Bend wings under the body with twine. Tie the legs together. Place stuffed goose, breast-side up, in an open roasting pan. Cover the breast with bacon strips.

Roast the goose at 325 degrees for 2½ hours. Baste frequently with the pan juices. Sprinkle generously with Cassis liqueur and cook for another 10 minutes.

Serve with Plum Sauce: In a medium saucepan, slowly heat the wine for 2 to 3 minutes. Add the pan drippings and cook for another 3 minutes. Crush the plums slightly with a fork and add them to the wine mixture along with the cinnamon and cayenne. Simmer for another 5 minutes.

In a small bowl, combine the cornstarch with 2 tablespoons water, stir it to make a smooth paste, and add it to the plum mixture.

Bring the mixture to a boil, stirring constantly. Reduce heat and simmer. Stir occasionally for about 20 minutes, until sauce is thickened and translucent. You should have 3 cups Plum Sauce.

Serves 6.

CARVING INSTRUCTIONS

It is much easier to carve a whole game bird than a domestic fowl such as turkey, primarily because the game bird is so much smaller. You do not have to bother with elaborate carving procedures for the drumstick and thigh, since the leg of a game bird—even large game

such as wild goose — is comparatively small; simply remove the entire drumstick in a single piece. You do not
even have to be concerned with carving the wings, since
the wings of game birds are generally removed before
cooking, as they are the toughest part of the meat.

When your beautifully prepared, lusciously aromatic
bird has been cooked to perfection, place it on a heated
platter large enough to give the carver elbow room. If
the bird has been stuffed, remove all the stuffing and
place it in an attractive heated serving bowl before carving the bird. Have ready a very sharp carving knife and a
long-handled two-tined fork, also an extra serving platter
for the carved pieces to be placed upon for passing to
your hungry guests.

GEESE AND PHEASANT: First, turn the bird on
its side with the breastbone away from you. Hold the
drumstick with your left hand or a fork stuck firmly
into its center. Pull the drumstick away from the body

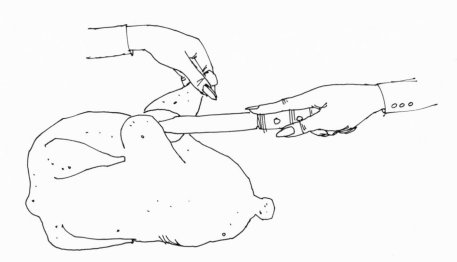

as you cut through the joint with your knife. Twist the knife slightly as you cut to sever the tendons. Place the drumstick on the serving platter and then remove the other drumstick. You are now ready to carve the breast.

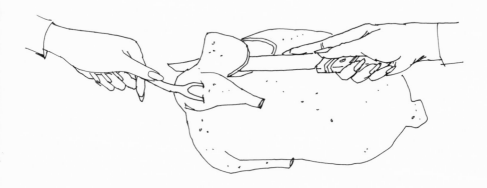

When carving large domestic birds, you generally slice the breast meat against the grain. However, since game birds — even the larger species such as goose and pheasant — have comparatively less breast meat, we suggest you carve the breast along the grain. Slice it lengthwise until you reach the wing joint. Continue slicing until you have carved all the meat on one side of the breast, then repeat the procedure on the other side. Place on platter and serve.

DUCK AND OTHER SMALL BIRDS: Very small birds are generally served whole as a single portion per diner. If your bird is large enough to serve two people, split the bird in half lengthwise by cutting through the backbone with poultry shears.

A Fish
Out of Water

Much of the work involved in cleaning fish is generally done by the deckhands on a party fishing boat or by your sportsman himself. For those of you who are faced with the catch intact, *au naturel*, take heart. Cleaning fish isn't as bad as it's cut out to be.

The necessary tools are a fish scaler, a sharp knife, and a cutting board. We also suggest you use a generous quantity of newspaper to cover your work surfaces; this will lighten your tidying-up chores.

The first step should be scaling. However, if you plan to skin the fish, do not waste your time by scraping off the scales. Also, if you intend to fillet your fish, scale only but do not dress.

TO SCALE: Rinse the whole fish in cold water and then lay it on your cutting board. With one hand, firmly grasp the fish by its head. In your other hand, hold the fish scaler almost vertically and scrape off all the scales, working from tail to head.

TO DRESS: Slit open the entire length of the belly to remove the entrails. Next fin and trim the fish. The fish has five fins, which you will now remove. Using the sharp tip of your knife, cut around the anal and pelvic (ventral) fins and discard. To remove the dorsal fin, cut along the flesh on each side, taking care not to cut through the bone itself. Then grasp the fin firmly and pull it toward the head of the fish, removing the fin and

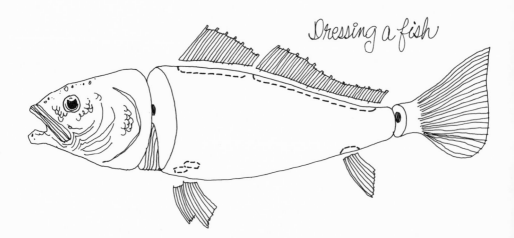

Dressing a fish

root bones at the same time. Place your knife behind the base of the pectoral fin and in one quick slicing motion across the collar bone (gill area) and through the backbone, sever both the pectoral fin and head. If you are dealing with a fish that has a large backbone, you may find it helpful to snap the bone on the edge of your cutting board. Last, cut off the tail (caudal) fin.

In some instances you may wish to keep the head and tail intact, since this lends eye appeal to certain fish dishes.

Unless you wish to cut it into steaks or chunks, skin or fillet it, your fish is now dressed and ready for freezing (see instructions, pages 18–23) or cooking.

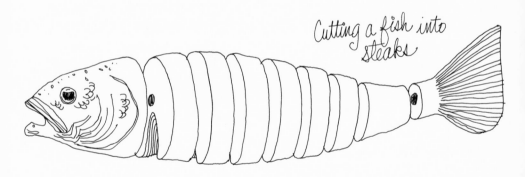

Cutting a fish into steaks

TO MAKE STEAKS: Cut across your dressed fish vertically through the backbone. How thick you cut them depends upon your preference—between one half and one full inch is best. Special attention must be given to albacore, since this is a strong, oily fish. The oils are concentrated along the backbone, which you'll notice as areas of dark-red meat. It is best to cut out these areas before cooking, otherwise the oil will impart a strong flavor to your fish. You can also remove the bones at this time. If your albacore appears to be falling apart, don't fret. Press the loose chunks of meat into the center of your steak. Although albacore is extremely soft in its raw state, the meat firms in cooking.

For soups, stews, or chowders, you will want to cut the fish into chunks from one to three inches in thickness.

TO SKIN: Depending upon your personal preference, you may wish to skin fish which are to be cooked whole. The necessary utensils are a sharp knife, a cutting board, and perhaps a pair of pliers if you are working with a large fish.

Lay the fish on the cutting board. At the head end of the fish, insert the tip of your knife between the skin and the flesh with one hand and grasp the loosened flap of skin with the other, slowly and firmly peeling back toward the tail end.

If the skin adheres to the flesh at any point, separate it again with your knife, then continue to peel. Large fish may be especially stubborn in refusing to shed their skin—this is when your pliers will come in handy. Use them to get a firm grasp, always being careful not to take the flesh away with the skin.

Having skinned one whole side of your fish, flop it over and repeat the process. The second side is always easier since you've gained in dexterity and experience.

TO FILLET: Start with a fish that has not been cleaned or trimmed. Take your sharp knife in hand and cut through the flesh along the backbone from behind

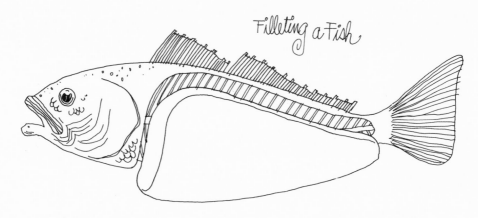

Filleting a Fish

the gills to the tail. The knife should barely touch the spine. (We prefer working in the gill-to-tail direction, filleting mainly the prime meat, since the belly meat is less tasty.) Now turn the knife flat against the spine. Separate the meat from the bone, maneuvering the knife in a lengthwise direction.

You now have one whole fillet. Turn the fish over and repeat the filleting process.

TO SKIN A FISH FILLET: Lay the fillet flat on your cutting board, flesh-side up. Gently slice down to the skin at the tail end of the fish. Grasping the skin with your fingers, turn the blade of your knife to a horizontal position and carefully cut the flesh away from the skin. As you slowly move the knife toward the head end, pull the skin away with your other hand.

Your decision to skin depends upon taste preference and recipe selection.

Now that your fish is scaled, trimmed, filleted, or cut into steaks, chunks, or whatever, we suggest you DO NOT REWASH your fish if you plan to freeze it (see freez-

ing instructions, pages 18–23). We picked up this hint in Ensenada, Mexico, from the deckhands who so professionally cleaned our day's catch. It seems that too much water just washes away the flavor and natural juices. When you are ready to prepare your fish for cooking, THEN you should quickly dip it in cold, salted water and pat it dry with a paper towel.

That strong, fishy odor on your utensils and hands is inescapable. What to do about it? Your first impulse may be to run for a bar of soap. Don't.

Make a strong solution of ordinary kitchen salt and warm water. Soak all utensils used in preparing fish in this solution, rinse, then wash with cleanser and warm water.

For your hands, make a paste of salt moistened with water. Rub this all over your hands, working it deeply into the skin to remove the fish oils, then rinse and wash with soapy water. If odor stubbornly persists, cut a lemon and rub it over your hands. Wash again. If the odor still persists, treat yourself to a professional manicure.

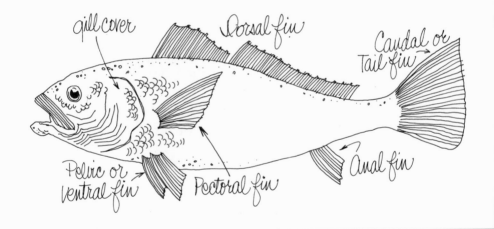

Rising to the Bait

We like to think of fish cookery as quick meal magic, since you can whip up a marvelous entrée generally within 30 minutes. Whether you prefer your fish *au naturel*, in sauce, fried, barbecued, whatever, there are a multitude of preparations to satisfy the most demanding taste buds.

Here are some of our favorites:

Simple Fish Poaching

Desired fish, fillets, or steaks
Simple poaching liquid (milk, cream, wine, tomato juice, canned soup such as shrimp or lobster bisque or cream of any vegetable)

Fill a frying pan or casserole one inch deep with any of the above choice of liquids. Cover and simmer the fish on the stove or in a 400-degree oven for approximately 15 minutes.

Basic Fish Poaching
(TOP-OF-RANGE METHOD)

Desired fish
1 onion, sliced
1 stalk celery, cut into chunks
1 carrot, sliced into rounds
2 bay leaves
3 whole black peppers
½ teaspoon salt
4 tablespoons lemon juice
½ cup dry white wine (optional)

If you do not have a special poaching pan, poach as follows: Use a large covered saucepan (select a pan according to the size of the fish). Combine all the ingredients in the pan with about a quart of water, or enough to just cover the fish (but do not add the fish yet). Bring the mixture to a boil. Reduce the heat and allow the liquid to simmer for 20 minutes.

Wipe the fish with a damp paper towel. Completely wrap the fish in a large piece of cheesecloth (it should extend a few inches past both ends of fish). Lower the fish into the simmering liquid, bringing the ends of the cheesecloth slightly over edge of pan for easy removal of the fish. Cover the pan and simmer the fish. Fish cooks quickly by this method, especially small fillets and steaks, so start checking for doneness after 5 minutes.

Large whole fish or large fish fillets require approximately 8 to 10 minutes per pound. When the fish flakes easily, carefully remove it from the liquid, still in its cheesecloth wrapping. Set it on a platter and allow it to drain before removing the cheesecloth. Strain the poaching liquid and reserve it for cooking stock—this is known as court-bouillon. You can store containers of court-bouillon in your freezer for later use.

Poached fish can be served hot or chilled; garnish with sliced lemon, fresh parsley, and your favorite sauce.

Basic Fish Poaching
(OVEN METHOD)

Desired fish fillet or
  chunk
1/2 cup white wine
  vinegar or lemon juice
1 teaspoon salt
1 bay leaf
1 onion, sliced

1 carrot, cut in rounds
2 sprigs parsley
6 whole black
  peppercorns
1 whole allspice
1/2 cup dry white
  wine (optional)

To poach a fillet or small chunk of fish, first wrap it in cheesecloth and then arrange it in a greased baking pan. Combine the poaching ingredients with about a quart of water in a large pot and simmer for at least 20 minutes. Bring it to a boil and pour it over the fish. Cover and place the fish in a preheated 425-degree oven. Cook until the fish flakes easily when tested with a fork. The approximate poaching time for small fish is 6 to 8 minutes. Large loins of albacore (boneless section of solid white meat) take at least 20 minutes.

When poached, remove the fish from the baking pan with a wide spatula. Drain well and unwrap the cheesecloth. Strain the court-bouillon and reserve it for future use in recipe preparations. Quantities may be stored in your freezer.

Chilled Poached Albacore with Cucumber Sauce

1 albacore fillet, about
  2½ pounds

Basic Poaching Liquid
  (*see* page 104)

Cucumber Sauce:
3 long, thin cucumbers
2 teaspoons salt
1 cup sour cream

1 cup mayonnaise
1 tablespoon chopped
  fresh dill

Follow the Basic Fish Poaching recipe for albacore fillet (pages 104–5). Chill the poached fillet.

To make the Cucumber Sauce: Peel the cucumbers, cut them in half, and discard the seeds. Then finely chop them and sprinkle with salt. Chill for at least 2 hours. Drain and mix the cucumbers with the sour cream, mayonnaise, and chopped fresh dill. Serve with the chilled albacore fillet.

Serves 4.

Barbecued Albacore Steaks

4 albacore steaks, ½ inch
  thick
½ cup melted butter

½ cup fresh lemon juice
3 tablespoons sherry or
  vermouth (optional)

Wash the fish and dry with a paper towel. Combine the butter and lemon juice, also the sherry or vermouth if used. Brush both sides of fish with the baste. Place the fish on a greased barbecue grill over coals. Barbecue the steaks for about 7 minutes on each side, basting frequently, or until the fish flakes easily.

Serves 4.

Albacore Olé

3 fillets white meat albacore, about 2 pounds each
6 medium onions, thickly sliced
3 large green peppers, cut into large pieces
1 large clove garlic, split
¼ cup oil

4 large tomatoes, cut into large pieces
3 yellow chiles, diced
1 large green chile, diced
3 8-ounce cans tomato sauce
8-ounce can *chile salsa*
Salt, pepper, and chili powder to taste

Sauté the onions, green peppers, and garlic in oil until soft. Arrange the albacore in a large baking pan. Add the sautéed vegetables, tomatoes, chiles, tomato and chile sauces, and salt, pepper, and chili powder to taste. Cover and bake at 350 degrees for 2 hours. Check occasionally; if the sauce is too thick, add water.

Serves 8 to 10.

For the busy cook, this dish can be put together in the morning and then baked in the evening. Also, since it requires no basting or checking, you can put it in the oven and then do other projects while it safely and deliciously cooks.

Albacore in Onion Soup Sauce

1 albacore fillet,
  approximately 2½
  pounds
Salt, pepper, and garlic
  powder
1 package prepared onion
  soup mix

1 cup white wine
  (Sauterne)
Paprika (in generous
  proportions)

Wash the albacore and dry it with a paper towel. Place the fillet on a large piece of heavy-duty aluminum foil. Season with salt, pepper, and garlic powder. Now turn the edges of foil as if to make a bowl. Add the package of onion soup mix, pour in the wine, and sprinkle generously with paprika. Seal tightly and wrap in additional foil. Bake in a 350-degree oven for about 1½ to 2 hours, or until the fish flakes when fork-tested.

Serves 4.

Albacore Iced Like a Cake

2-pound albacore fillet
2 8-ounce containers sour
  cream
1 tablespoon toasted
  onion flakes
3 tablespoons white
  cream-style horseradish

1 teaspoon dry mustard
½ lemon
Salt and pepper
2 large pimiento pieces,
  each cut in half
Parsley
Lemon slices

In a mixing bowl, combine the sour cream, onion flakes, horseradish, and mustard. Place a quarter of the sour-cream mixture on the bottom of a deep baking pan. Rub the albacore with the lemon and season with salt and pepper.

Spread the remaining sour-cream mixture over the albacore as though you were icing a cake. Decorate with the pimiento. Cover with aluminum foil and bake at 400 degrees for 1½ to 2 hours. When you serve, place the fillet in the center of a platter and repair any "icing" that may have run down. Garnish with parsley and lemon slices.

Serves 4.

Herbed Albacore Barbecue

1 firm albacore fillet, about 3 pounds	½ teaspoon each of rosemary, oregano, and thyme
½ cup oil	
1 lemon, cut into wedges	

Sherry-Soy Baste:

⅔ cup sherry	Juice of 1 lemon
⅓ cup soy sauce	Dash of powdered thyme

Combine all the ingredients for the Sherry-Soy Baste. Rub the fish with the oil, lemon wedges, and herbs. Place the fillet on a greased grill over hot coals. Turn as necessary, always basting with Sherry-Soy Baste. Press the fish to check for doneness. Do not overcook the albacore; it is preferable to have it barely done in the center. The approximate barbecuing time, depending upon the thickness of the fillet, is 8 to 10 minutes per side.

Serves 6 to 8.

A good dip to accompany the fish is:

Dill Dip

²/₃ cup sour cream
²/₃ cup mayonnaise
1 tablespoon dillweed
1 tablespoon shredded
  parsley
1 tablespoon chopped

scallions (green onions)
1 teaspoon *Beau Monde*
  (optional)
½ dill pickle, finely
  minced

Combine the above ingredients. Prepare well ahead of time so that the flavors blend. Refrigerate. When serving, pass with the fish.

Hawaiian-Sesame Albacore

4 albacore steaks
  approximately 8 ounces
  each
1 cup teriyaki marinade
  (bottled or
  homemade—*see* page 27)

8 strips bacon
½ cup butter
Juice of 2 lemons
¼ cup sherry
¼ cup sesame seeds

Wash the albacore and dry with a paper towel. Place the steaks in a dish with ½ cup of the teriyaki marinade and refrigerate for 1 hour.

To prepare for barbecue: Wrap each piece with 2 strips of bacon and fasten with toothpicks. This not only keeps the fish neatly together but also adds extra flavor and juiciness. As soon as the fish begins to cook, the meat firms and can be easily handled.

In a small pan, melt the butter and remove it from the heat. Stir in the remaining ½ cup teriyaki marinade, lemon juice, and sherry. Arrange the fish on the barbecue grill over medium-hot coals. Brush well with the baste.

When the steaks are done on one side, sprinkle with sesame seeds, turn over, and cook until the other side is brown. Now baste and sprinkle again with sesame seeds. Before serving, turn the steaks over once more to toast all the seeds. The total barbecuing time should be about 15 minutes. Garnish with lemon wedges.

Serves 4.

This is a rare delicacy for the educated palate.

Albacore Sashimi

¾ pound *fresh* albacore
  fillet
½ lemon
2 tablespoons Japanese
  horseradish powder (if
  unable to obtain use

dry hot mustard)
Dash of vinegar
½ cup soy sauce
4 pairs chopsticks
  (optional)

Slice the albacore into the thinnest strips possible, then cut each strip in half (this should give you at least 20 pieces). Squeeze the juice of ½ lemon on top of the fish and place the fish on a serving platter. Put the horseradish powder in a small serving bowl. Slowly add hot water, a few drops at a time, stirring until the powder forms a paste. Add a dash of vinegar, cover, and let stand for 5 to 6 minutes. Pour soy sauce into a separate serving bowl.

If you have never eaten Sashimi, this is how: Pick up a slice of raw fish with your chopsticks. Dip the fish first in soy sauce, then in horseradish sauce. Serve with bowl of cooked, hot white rice.

You can also make Sashimi with yellowtail tuna, sea bass, or any raw fish of your preference.

Serves 4 to 6.

If you are not familiar with the taste, feel, or look of barracuda, its texture and flavor is similar to dark meat tuna.

Barracuda Italiano

4 barracuda steaks, about
  ¾ inch thick
1 cup Italian salad

dressing (basically oil,
vinegar, basil, garlic,
salt, and pepper)

Marinate the fish in the refrigerator in Italian salad dressing for 2 to 4 hours. Punch holes in a piece of heavy-duty aluminum foil and place it on the barbecue grill. Barbecue the fish on the foil for 8 to 10 minutes, turning once and basting often with marinade.

Serves 4.

Mahimahi is generally found in tropical waters and is a favorite dish in Hawaii. Mahimahi is the Hawaiian word for dolphin.

Pan-Fried Mahimahi

1½ pounds mahimahi
  (dolphin) fillet skinned
½ cup milk
4 tablespoons pancake
  flour
Salt, pepper, and dry

mustard
4 tablespoons butter
3 tablespoons lemon
  juice
2 tablespoons chopped
  fresh parsley

Dip the fillet in milk, then dredge in pancake flour. Season the fillet with salt, pepper, and dry mustard. Melt the butter in a skillet and lightly fry the fillet on one side until the coating is golden color (approximately 6 minutes). Turn over with wide spatula and fry other side for about another 6 minutes, or until the fish flakes easily.

Remove the fish to a heated serving platter. Stir the lemon juice and parsley into the butter remaining in the skillet. Pour the sauce over the fish and serve immediately.

Serves 4.

The following recipe is fit for a king.

Mahimahi with Puff Crown

1½ pounds mahimahi
  (dolphin) fillet
1½ cups milk
3 tablespoons butter
½ cup mayonnaise
2 tablespoons lemon
  juice
¼ teaspoon salt
¼ teaspoon pepper

½ teaspoon dry mustard
1 teaspoon toasted onion
  flakes
1 teaspoon capers
2 teaspoons grated
  Parmesan cheese
2 egg whites
Dash of paprika

Remove the skin from the mahimahi fillet. Pour the milk into a shallow bowl, put fillet in the bowl, cover, and refrigerate for 30 minutes, turning once. Remove the fish from the milk and discard the milk. Melt the butter in a baking dish and turn the fillet in the melted butter to coat both sides. Place the baking dish under the broiler and broil for about 8 minutes or until the fillet is nearly done.

While the fish is broiling, make the topping by combining in a mixing bowl the mayonnaise, lemon juice, salt, pepper, mustard, onion flakes, capers, and Parmesan cheese. Beat the egg whites until stiff and fold them into the topping mixture. Spread the topping generously on the fillet and sprinkle with paprika. Broil until the crown topping is puffed up and golden color.

Serves 4.

Mahimahi del Sol

1½ pounds mahimahi (dolphin) fillet, skinned
Salt, pepper, and paprika
4 tablespoons butter
2 shallots, minced

1 bay leaf, crushed
3 tablespoons lemon juice
½ cup toasted sliced filberts (optional)

Wipe the fish with a damp paper towel. Sprinkle salt, pepper, and paprika on the fillet. Melt the butter in a saucepan, add the shallots, bay leaf, and lemon juice, then stir and remove the pan from the heat. Brush the fish heavily with the butter mixture. Place the fish on a greased rack under the broiler. Broil for 5 minutes on one side, turn the fillet, and brush heavily with the butter baste. Broil for another 5 minutes, or until the fish flakes easily.

If you choose to garnish with sliced filberts (sliced almonds may also be used), pour the remaining butter baste into a skillet, add the sliced nuts, bring to high heat, and quickly sauté until the nuts are golden color. Pour the nuts and pan drippings over the fish and serve immediately.

Serves 4.

Sesame-Baked Mahimahi

1 ½ pounds mahimahi
  (dolphin) fillet, skinned
2 eggs
2 tablespoons milk
½ teaspoon each of salt,
  pepper, and dry

mustard
1 tablespoon lemon juice
½ cup flour
1 cup sesame seeds
6 tablespoons melted
  butter

Beat the eggs lightly and blend in the milk, salt, pepper, dry mustard, and lemon juice. Dip the fish into the egg mixture, then dredge very lightly in flour. Dip the fish into the egg mixture again, then place it firmly on a shallow layer of sesame seeds, pressing all sides of the fish into seeds until well coated.

Place the fish in a baking dish with 4 tablespoons of the melted butter. Pour the remaining butter on top of the fish. Bake at 375 degrees for 15 minutes, turn over, and bake for another 10 minutes.

Serves 4.

Mahimahi in Dilled Mushroom Sauce

1 ½ pounds mahimahi
  (dolphin) fillet
½ teaspoon salt
½ teaspoon pepper
2 tablespoons butter
½ cup condensed cream
  of mushroom soup

½ cup sour cream
1 teaspoon dillweed
½ teaspoon dry mustard
1 teaspoon capers

Remove the skin from the fillet. Season the fish with salt and pepper and place it in a greased baking dish. Dot the top of the fish with the butter. Bake at 375 degrees for 10 to 15 minutes, or until the fish flakes easily when tested with a fork.

While the fish is baking, combine the mushroom soup, sour cream, dillweed, and dry mustard and stir until blended. About 2 to 3 minutes before the fish is done, remove it from the oven and spread the dilled mushroom sauce over the top. Heat under the broiler for 2 to 3 minutes until the sauce is glazed and slightly browned. Sprinkle the capers over the top and serve immediately.

Serves 4.

Mandarin Orange Mahimahi

2 pounds mahimahi (dolphin) fillet
6-ounce can frozen orange-pineapple juice concentrate thawed
12 ounces ginger ale
1 teaspoon soy sauce
¼ teaspoon each of salt and pepper
11-ounce can mandarin orange segments (with syrup)
2 tablespoons butter

Dilute the juice concentrate with ginger ale. Combine with the soy sauce, salt, and pepper. Drain the syrup from the can of mandarin oranges, set orange segments aside, and add syrup to juice mixture.

Remove the skin from the fish. Place the fish in a shallow dish, pour half the juice mixture over the fish, reserving the other half for the orange garnish. Let the fish marinate in the juice at room temperature for 30 minutes; turn once. Remove the fish from the marinade and put it in a lightly buttered baking dish. Dot the top with butter bits. Bake at 375 degrees for 15 to 20 minutes or until done; the time needed will depend on the thickness of the fillet. During the last few minutes of the baking, add the orange segments to the remaining juice mixture and heat slowly in a saucepan. Pour the garnish over the fish just before serving.

Serves 4 to 6.

The secret to this tasty dish is not to overcook the pompano fillet, since it is quite thin.

Flash-in-the-Pan Pompano

1½ pounds pompano fillet, skinned and cut into 4 pieces
1 egg, beaten with a little water
⅓ cup seasoned bread crumbs

2 tablespoons grated Parmesan cheese
½ teaspoon dry mustard
2 shallots, sliced thin
4 tablespoons butter

Dip the fish in the egg, then in bread crumbs mixed with the Parmesan cheese and mustard. In a large frypan, sauté shallots in butter until golden, then remove the shallots. Put the fish in a single layer in the frypan and sauté until golden on one side (about 4 to 5 minutes). Turn over with a wide spatula so that the thin fillets do not break. Sauté on other side for 4 to 5 minutes, until fish flakes easily. Place on a heated serving platter, pour the pan drippings over the fish, and serve immediately.

Serves 4.

The traditional way to prepare pompano is in individual parchment or waxed paper "envelopes" known as papillotes. *While cooking, the* papillotes *puff up and the pompano inside steams in its own sauce.*

Pompano en Papillotes

1½ pounds pompano
  fillets, cut into 4
  servings
3 tablespoons flour
  seasoned with salt and
  pepper
3 tablespoons butter
½ lemon

2 shallots, sliced
Flour (to thicken sauce)
¼ cup white wine
4 tablespoons chopped
  mushrooms
1½ cups court-bouillon
  (*see* below or pages 104–5)
Salt and pepper to taste

Lightly dredge the pompano fillets in the seasoned flour. Pan-fry the fillets quickly in butter until golden (about 2 minutes on each side), turning with wide spatula so that fish does not fall apart. Squeeze the juice of the lemon over fillets, remove them from the pan and set aside on a heated platter.

Sauté the shallots until golden in the same pan used to fry fillets. Remove the shallots and stir enough flour into the pan drippings to make a fairly thick paste. Then add the wine, mushrooms, and court-bouillon. (You can make a nice court-bouillon by combining in a pot the bone from the pompano with 2 cups water, 2 bay leaves, and 1 sliced onion. Bring to a boil, reduce heat, and simmer for ½ hour, then strain.) Season the sauce in the frypan to taste with salt and pepper. Remove from the heat.

To make your *papillotes:* For each serving, take regular waxed paper or parchment paper about 12 inches long and fold it in half lengthwise. Cut a heart shape as large as possible. Butter both sides of the paper. On the inside, place one serving of fish on one half of the heart.

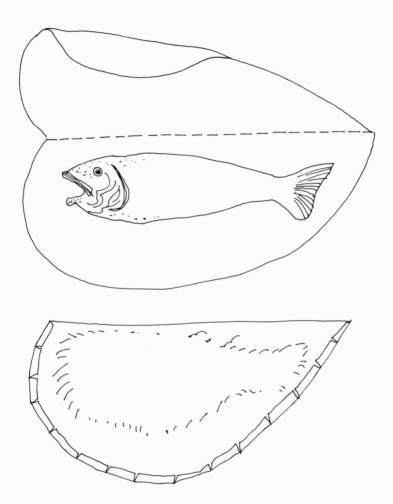

Spoon the sauce on top of fish. Fold paper over the fish and, starting at the inside of the heart, fold the paper over a half inch and crease, again and again, at half-inch intervals all around, completely sealing in the fish and sauce.

Place the *papillotes* in a shallow baking dish and bake for 20 minutes at 350 degrees. When ready to serve, a *papillote* is placed on each diner's dish.

Serves 4.

Fast Salmon Broil

4 salmon steaks
4 tablespoons French
　salad dressing
2 tablespoons soy sauce

½ teaspoon ground
　ginger
1 lime, cut into thin
　slices

Combine the salad dressing, soy sauce, and ginger. Place the fish on a cookie sheet. Brush sauce on both sides of the fish and let stand for about 5 minutes. Broil for 6 minutes, then gently turn fish over. Brush with any remaining sauce and broil on second side for 4 to 6 minutes, or until fish flakes when tested with a fork. Garnish with lime slices.

Serves 4.

Oven-Baked Fresh Salmon

An 8-pound salmon,
　cleaned
Salt and pepper
1 lemon

1 cup white wine
2 onions, 2 tomatoes, and
　2 oranges, all cut into
　thick rings

Place the salmon under cold running water for a moment and then pat it dry with a paper towel. Rub inside the cavity with salt, pepper, the juice of the lemon, and ¼ cup of the wine. Stuff the cavity with the onion, tomato, and orange slices, arranged in layers. Tie the fish together with thread and lay it in a large baking dish. Pour in the remaining wine. Bake at 350 degrees for about 45 minutes, or until the fish flakes easily when tested with a fork. Check occasionally to baste with pan liquids so that the skin doesn't dry out. When done, cut the thread and discard the orange slices. Keep the vegetable stuffing.

Serves 6 generously.

Polynesian Marinated Salmon

6 salmon steaks
12-ounce bottle teriyaki
 sauce (or homemade—
 see page 27)
½ teaspoon cinnamon

8-ounce can pineapple
 juice
Lemon or lime, cut into
 wedges

Combine the teriyaki sauce, pineapple juice, and cinnamon. Lay the salmon in a glass pyrex dish and pour the marinade on top. Cover and refrigerate for 3 hours.

Remove the steaks from the marinade and broil or barbecue for about 10 minutes, turning them once. Occasionally baste the fish with the marinade. Garnish with lemon or lime wedges.

Serves 6.

Mediterranean-Style Salmon Steaks

2 salmon steaks
8-ounce can tomato sauce
½ teaspoon oregano
¼ teaspoon garlic
 powder

¼ teaspoon salt
½ teaspoon pepper
1 medium-size onion,
 diced and sautéed

Wipe the salmon steaks with a damp paper towel and then pat dry. Place each steak on a piece of aluminum foil large enough to wrap the steak in. Combine the tomato sauce, oregano, garlic powder, salt, and pepper. Pour the sauce over the fish and top with the sautéed onion. Fold the foil over the top and sides of each steak, completely sealing in the sauce. Bake at 350 degrees for about 20 minutes, or until the fish flakes easily.

Serves 2.

Chilled Poached Salmon Stuffed with Cauliflower Rarebit

6- to 8-pound whole
poached salmon, boned
3 10-ounce packages
frozen cauliflower
1 can condensed Cheddar
cheese soup
1/2 cup beer
2 teaspoons
Worcestershire sauce

1 1/2 teaspoons dry
mustard
1/2 teaspoon pepper
3/4 cup cashew halves
1/2 pound cherry tomatoes
for garnish (optional)
Parsley or watercress
for garnish (optional

Cook the cauliflower according to the package directions, then drain and chill. In a mixing bowl, combine the soup and beer and stir until blended. Add the Worcestershire sauce, mustard, and pepper; stir. Cut the cauliflower into bite-size pieces of about 1 inch diameter. Add the cauliflower and cashew halves to soup mixture. Stuff the salmon with this mixture, reserving any leftovers for stuffing the cherry tomatoes. Chill until you are ready to serve.

To prepare the cherry tomato garnish: With the sharp point of a knife, cut into the top of each tomato and make a cavity, removing the pulp and seeds. Turn the tomatoes upside down on paper toweling and allow the juice to drain for a few minutes. Stuff each tomato cavity with the leftover cheese-cauliflower mixture. Arrange them attractively around fish with parsley or watercress.

Serves 12 to 15.

Salmon Stuffed with Shrimp

An 8- to 10-pound
  salmon, cleaned
Soy sauce
Tabasco
Salt and pepper
2 cups prepared poultry
  stuffing

1 cup cooked shrimp
Several lemons
3 tablespoons chicken
  stock
3 tablespoons white wine

Rub the cavity of the fish with soy sauce and a few drops of tabasco. Salt and pepper the outside lightly. Mix the prepared poultry stuffing with the cooked shrimp and add the juice of ½ lemon.

Moisten the dressing with equal parts chicken stock and wine so that dressing holds together without becoming mushy. Place the fish on its side, with the cavity towards you, on a piece of heavy-duty aluminum foil large enough to completely wrap and seal fish.

Fill the cavity with dressing, heaping in as much as it will hold. Loosely wrap the foil around fish and seal. Bake the salmon in a 350-degree oven or place it on a charcoal grill. When barbecuing, keep the coals a distance from the grill to prevent burning fish. The salmon is done when it indents easily when outside of foil is pinched (this should take about 30 minutes). When the foil package is opened, remove the dressing to a serving bowl and garnish with lemon wedges.

Serves 8 to 10.

Salmon Stuffed with Crabmeat

A 7- to 10-pound salmon,
  cleaned (steelhead
  trout can be
  substituted)
1 lemon, cut in half
1 pound crab meat
  (preferably fresh;
  canned can be
  substituted)
¼ cup chopped chives
¼ cup chopped parsley

3 tablespoons finely
  chopped celery
¼ cup melted butter
½ cup bread crumbs
¼ cup mayonnaise
Freshly ground black
  pepper
¾ cup dry white wine
  (Sauterne)
Salt

Rub the inside of the salmon with lemon. In a large
mixing bowl, combine the crab meat, chives, parsley,
celery, butter, bread crumbs, mayonnaise, and a dash of

pepper. Stuff the fish with this mixture and gently close with string or thick thread.

Lay the fish lengthwise on a long sheet of heavy-duty aluminum foil. Bring up the edges of foil and pour the wine over the fish. Season with salt. Completely enclose the fish, crimping and folding the foil to seal the edges tightly. Place the foil-wrapped fish in a large baking pan and transfer to the oven. Bake at 375 degrees for 1 to 1½ hours, until the fish flakes easily.

Serves 12 to 15.

Salmon Under Wraps

A 10-pound salmon,
   cleaned and skinned
Salt and pepper
1 lemon
1-pound-12-ounce can
   peeled whole tomatoes
   (with juice)

1-pound can stewed
   tomatoes
1-pound can tomato sauce
   with onions
1 large onion, cut into
   large chunks
4 sprigs parsley, shredded

Place the salmon in an aluminum roasting pan. Season with salt and pepper and the juice of 1 lemon. Add the canned tomatoes (with juice), stewed tomatoes, tomato sauce, onion, and parsley.

Push together the four sides of the aluminum pan toward the fish. Wrap entire pan, top and bottom, twice with foil. Place the sealed package on the grill on top of very hot barbecue coals. Barbecue for approximately 30 minutes.

Serves at least 8.

Cold Poached Salmon Fillet in Glazed Aspic

A 3-pound salmon fillet,
    poached and chilled
²/₃ cup sour cream
⅓ cup creamed white
    horseradish
2 tablespoons lemon
    juice
2 envelopes unflavored

gelatin
1½ cups court-bouillon
    (reserved from
    poaching liquid)
Your choice of
    decorations: capers,
    chives, pimiento, sliced
    black olives

To make the aspic: Combine the sour cream, horse-radish, and lemon juice. Soften 1 package gelatin in ¼ cup court-bouillon. Beat the softened gelatin into the sour-cream mixture; set aside.

In order to attain a neat, professional-looking glaze, triple-fold heavy-duty aluminum foil to the width of your fillet, allowing length to extend a few inches beyond the fillet. Lightly oil the top surface of the foil. Place the poached, chilled salmon on the foil, place the foil on a wire rack, and set the rack on a platter. Spread the aspic over the cold salmon with a spatula (the excess will fall through the rack onto the platter). Refrigerate until the aspic is set.

Meanwhile, soften the second package of gelatin in ¼ cup of the court-bouillon. Heat the remaining court-bouillon, add it to the softened gelatin, and stir until completely dissolved. Cool the gelatin until it is the consistency of raw egg white. This will be your glaze. When the sour cream—horseradish aspic is set, decorate as desired, first dipping the decorations in the gelatin glaze. Refrigerate until decorations are set on the aspic.

Pour two layers of gelatin glaze over the aspic, chilling between each layer until the glaze is set.

When ready to serve, lift the glazed salmon with the foil onto a serving platter. Insert a wide spatula under one end of the salmon and slide the foil out. Garnish the platter with pickled cauliflower and pickled carrots.

Serves 6.

Turn leftover fish into gala dining with a fluffy soufflé.

Salmon Soufflé

1 ¼ cups flaked cooked salmon	1 tablespoon sherry
3 tablespoons butter (plus extra for greasing the baking dish)	Dash each of salt, pepper, paprika, and Worcestershire sauce
3 tablespoons flour	¼ teaspoon dry mustard
1 cup milk	¼ cup finely diced onion
4 eggs	1 tablespoon chopped pimiento

Since a fluffy soufflé depends on timing, we suggest you first preheat your oven to 375 degrees. Prepare your soufflé dish or 2-quart baking casserole by greasing it well with butter. Put water up to boil and have ready a shallow pan to set soufflé or baking dish in. Now you are ready to start your soufflé.

Melt the butter in a deep saucepan. Slowly add the flour, stirring with a wooden spoon until the mixture is smooth. In a separate pan, heat the milk just to a boil. Add the milk to the butter-and-flour mixture, stirring rapidly with wooden spoon or wire whisk until smooth. You now have a basic white sauce. Set it aside to cool.

Separate the egg yolks from the whites and set aside the whites. Use only 3 of the yolks (you'll get a fluffier soufflé by using 4 egg whites to 3 egg yolks). Beat the yolks into the white sauce, add the sherry, salt, pepper, paprika, Worcestershire sauce, and dry mustard. Stir rapidly so that sauce remains smooth. Add the flaked salmon, onion, and pimiento and mix thoroughly into sauce.

Beat the egg whites until stiff, then fold (do not beat) into the salmon soufflé mixture. Pour the entire mixture into the greased baking dish, set the dish in the shallow pan, and place in the oven. Pour boiling water in the pan to a depth of ¼ inch. Bake the soufflé for about 40 to 45 minutes, until done. Serve immediately with your favorite sauce, or try this one:

Easy Celery Sauce:

10¾-ounce can
  condensed cream of
  celery soup
½ cup milk
½ cup sherry

Dash of Worcestershire
  sauce
¼ cup cooked baby
  shrimp (optional)

Combine all the ingredients except the shrimp in a saucepan, stir until smooth, and heat. Just before serving, add the shrimp, stir, and heat for a moment longer.

Soufflé and sauce serves 3.

Salmon Mousse

2 cups chilled poached
  salmon, finely flaked
1 tablespoon unflavored
  gelatin
¼ cup cold court-
  bouillon (*see* page 118)
½ cup boiling court-
  bouillon
⅔ cup mayonnaise

½ teaspoon each of salt
  and pepper
¾ teaspoon dry mustard
3 tablespoons lemon
  juice
1 tablespoon
  Worcestershire sauce
¼ cup pickle relish
⅓ cup heavy cream

Soften the gelatin in the cold court-bouillon, then add the boiling court-bouillon, and stir until the gelatin is completely dissolved. Set aside to cool.

In a mixing bowl, combine the mayonnaise, salt, pepper, mustard, lemon juice, and Worcestershire sauce. Stir in the cooled gelatin. Chill until the mixture has the consistency of an unbeaten egg white. Combine the salmon and relish and add to the chilled mayonnaise mixture. Whip the heavy cream until it is stiff, then fold it into the salmon mixture. Turn the mixture into an oiled quart-size mold. Refrigerate the mousse until it is set. Unmold it on a serving platter, garnish with salad greens and wafer-thin slices of lemon and lime.

Serves 6.

Halibut Ahoy

4 halibut steaks, about ½
   inch thick
Salt and pepper to taste
2 cups milk

4 slices sandwich cheese
   (round Cheddar or
   American)

Place the halibut in a single layer in a baking dish. Cover generously with salt and pepper. Top with cheese slices. Pour milk on top to almost cover fish. Bake for about 30 minutes at 350 degrees, or until the fish flakes easily.

Serves 4.

Pork-Stuffed Halibut

1 halibut, cleaned
   (approximately 9 to 10
   pounds)
3 onions
2 pounds bulk pork
   sausage

3 lemons
2 strips bacon
1½ cups Bordeaux wine
1-pound can of peeled
   tomatoes (with liquid)
1 teaspoon garlic salt

Wipe the fish with a damp paper towel. Stuff the cavity with 2 of the onions (coarsely chopped) and the sausage. Lace up the cavity. Place the fish in a large aluminum roasting pan. Thinly slice the remaining onion and 1 of the lemons and place them around the fish. Place the bacon strips over the fish. Squeeze the juice from the 2 remaining lemons into the pan. Add the wine, tomatoes (and their liquid), and garlic salt. Bake, uncovered, at 350 degrees for 1½ hours.

Other fish that taste delicious prepared this way are bonito, yellowtail, and sheepshead. To reduce gaminess, soak the cleaned fish in salted water for 8 hours.

Leftovers are excellent refrigerated and served chilled the next day.

Serves 8.

Halibut Anisette

1 pound halibut fillet (or
  any delicate white fish
  fillet)
½ medium-size cucumber
¾ teaspoon fennel seeds
  (substitute fresh fennel
  if available)

½ cup fresh watercress
½ cup anisette liqueur
Salt
2 wedges lemon

Wash the fish and pat it dry with a paper towel. Lay the fillet in a large baking pan. Peel and slice the cucumber into very thin wafers and place them on top of the fish. Crush the fennel seeds — or, if you use fresh fennel, tear the feathery top into very small pieces — and sprinkle on top of the cucumber wafers. Next, tear the watercress by hand and layer it over the fennel. Pour on the liqueur and season with salt. Squeeze one of the lemon wedges over the fish (this will cut the sweetness of the liqueur).

Bake at 350 degrees. After 5 minutes, check the fish and squeeze the second lemon wedge on top. Spoon the pan juices over the fish. Bake for another 5 to 8 minutes, or until the fish flakes when tested with a fork.

Serves 2.

Halibut Apritada
(PHILIPPINE STYLE)

2 pounds halibut fillet,
  cut into bite-size cubes
6 eggs

1 teaspoon salt
⅓ cup flour
Cooking oil

Beat the eggs with a wire whisk. Add the salt and flour and beat again with the whisk. Dip the halibut cubes into the batter until heavily coated. Pour oil in a large skillet to a 2-inch depth and heat until very hot. Place the fish cubes in a single layer in the hot oil (do not overlap). Fry the cubes on each side until they are golden-brown, then remove them from the oil and drain on a paper towel. Serve with the following sauce dip.

Apritada Dip:

2 tablespoons cooking oil
1 onion, sliced
⅓ cup tomato paste
⅓ cup liquid from jar of commercial sweet pickles
13 ¼-ounce can
pineapple tidbits
Flour
2 teaspoons sugar
½ cup chopped green pepper
1 carrot, sliced into wafer-thin rounds

Heat the oil in a frypan, sauté the onion, and add the tomato paste and ⅓ cup water. Then add the pickle juice and pineapple (with its juice). Thicken the sauce with a little flour. Stir in the sugar, green pepper, and carrot. Cook for 2 minutes over high heat. Pour it into an attractive serving bowl as a dip for the fried fish cubes.

Fish and dip serve 4 to 5.

Bouillabaisse

3 pounds assorted fish pieces (cod, bass, halibut, snapper)
½ cup butter
4 large onions, chopped
2 garlic cloves, minced
4 large tomatoes, chopped
2 bay leaves
1 sprig thyme
Salt and pepper to taste
2 cups wine (preferably red)

Melt the butter in a flameproof casserole large enough to hold all the ingredients and attractive enough to be placed directly on the dinner table. Add the chopped onion and garlic and sauté until golden (not brown). Then add the tomatoes and fish. Crumble the bay leaves and thyme directly into the casserole. Add salt and pepper. Finally, pour in the wine and 2 cups water and cover the casserole.

Simmer on the top of the stove for about 30 minutes. Occasionally check the amount of liquid; if needed, add more water and perhaps a touch more wine.

Serves 6 generously.

Cheese-Broiled Lingcod

1 ½ pounds lingcod fillet
½ cup butter
Salt, pepper, and mustard
   powder to taste

1 lemon
2 ounces crumbled blue
   cheese

Melt the butter and add the juice of 1 lemon. Pour a little of this mixture into a shallow ovenproof casserole. Season the fish with salt, pepper, and mustard powder and place it in the casserole. Spoon some of the butter-lemon baste over the fillet. Broil approximately 8 inches from the heat for 6 minutes, basting often. Turn the fish over and broil for another 5 minutes. Remove the fish from the broiler, top with the crumbled blue cheese, and return to the broiler for an additional minute, or until the cheese bubbles and melts.

Serves 4.

Tropical Baked Lingcod

4 lingcod fillets, 8 ounces
   each
½ lemon
1 cup light white wine
   (Chablis)

1 grapefruit
Dash of tabasco
2 sprigs cilantro (if
   unavailable substitute
   watercress)

Wipe the fillets with a damp paper towel. Rub lemon over the fillets and set aside. Peel the grapefruit and remove all the membrane. Cut the grapefruit into 1/8-inch thick slices, then cut each slice into 4 wedges.

Pour enough wine into the bottom of a casserole to form a thin layer of liquid. Place half the grapefruit wedges in a layer in the casserole. Place the fillets on top of the fruit. Sprinkle with a dash of tabasco (just enough for perk). Next, layer with cilantro leaves torn into small pieces by hand. Top with the remaining grapefruit wedges. Pour the remaining wine on top. Bake at 350 degrees for 18 minutes, or until fish flakes easily with a fork.

Serves 4.

Lingcod Snappy Style

8 small lingcod fillets
2 eggs, lightly beaten
Salt and pepper
1 envelope prepared chili
    sauce mix

Flour (optional)
4 tablespoons butter

Rinse the fillets and pat dry. Dip the fish in the beaten eggs to which salt and pepper have been added. Pour the envelope of chili sauce mix on waxed paper. If you wish, you may add a small amount of flour to extend the mix and to tone down the hot spice. Dredge the fish in the mix, coating evenly. Melt the butter and sauté the fish on both sides until the crust becomes crisp. The cooking time is approximately 10 minutes.

Serves 4.

In a rush? Try this:

Easy Sweet 'n' Sour Lingcod

1½ pounds lingcod, cut
    into 2-inch chunks
15-ounce can tomato
    sauce
1 cup tomato juice
Juice of 3½ lemons
1 clove

⅔ cup brown sugar,
    packed
⅓ cup white raisins,
    steeped and drained
1½ cups uncooked
    instant white rice

In a large casserole, combine all of the above ingredients and mix well. Cover and bake at 375 degrees for 18 minutes. Serve with a tossed green salad for a quick casserole dinner.

Serves 4.

Stuffed Lingcod Rollups

8 lingcod fillets, sliced 1/8
  inch thick
16 cocktail-size smoked
  link sausages
2 tablespoons butter
3 tablespoons chopped
  black olives

2 eggs, lightly beaten
2 tablespoons milk
1 cup bread crumbs
1/4 cup grated Parmesan
  cheese
Cooking oil

Wipe the fillets with a damp paper towel. Finely cut up the sausage and sauté in butter with the chopped olives until the sausage is cooked. Place 1/8 of the sausage-olive mixture on each fillet. Roll each fillet and secure all openings with toothpicks.

Dip each rollup into beaten eggs to which the milk has been added. Combine the bread crumbs and Parmesan cheese and pour into a paper bag. One at a time, shake the rollups in the paper bag until coated, then remove. Pour oil in a skillet to 1/2 inch depth. Heat. Fry rollups until golden and crusty on all sides and fish is tender (about 5 minutes). Place the fish on a paper towel to drain off oil.

Serves 4.

African Curried Lingcod

4 lingcod fillets (totaling
  approximately 1 1/2
  pounds)
1 pint buttermilk
1 tablespoon lemon juice
1 teaspoon salt

1/2 teaspoon tabasco sauce
1 teaspoon cumin seeds
3 tablespoons green
  pepper, finely chopped
1 teaspoon dry mustard
1/2 teaspoon curry powder

In a large skillet, combine the buttermilk, lemon juice, salt, and tabasco sauce. Bring to a boil and then reduce heat. Simmer for 10 minutes. Stir in the cumin seeds and chopped pepper.

Meanwhile, combine the dry mustard and curry powder. Sprinkle the mixture on the fillets and gently rub the spices into the fish. Place the fish in the buttermilk mixture and simmer for 10 to 12 minutes, or until the fish flakes easily. When serving, pour pan liquid over the fish.

Serves 4.

Having the gang over? Here's a great meal-in-one-pot.

Lingcod Vegetable Stew

3 pounds lingcod fillet, cut into 2-inch cubes
15-ounce can tomato sauce
16-ounce can whole peeled tomatoes
1/2 teaspoon salt
1/2 teaspoon pepper
1/4 teaspoon garlic powder

2 carrots, sliced into thin rounds
1 large onion, cut into chunks
4 large fresh mushrooms, sliced
1 small zucchini, sliced into thin rounds
1 cup uncooked white rice

In a large saucepan, combine the tomato sauce, whole tomatoes (with their liquid), 1/2 cup water, salt, pepper, and garlic powder. Add the carrots, onion, mushrooms, zucchini, and rice and stir. Add the fish cubes and mix with the sauce and vegetables. Cover the pot and place over medium heat. Cook for about 25 minutes (or until fish flakes easily), stirring occasionally. Serve with lots of crusty French bread and a good dry red wine.

Serves 8 to 10.

Cod Corn Chowder

1 ½ pounds lingcod, cut
   into large chunks
4 strips bacon, diced
4 tablespoons chopped
   onion
2 cups peeled and diced
   potatoes
1 quart milk

¼ teaspoon sage
Salt and pepper to taste
2 cups (2 8-ounce cans)
   cream-style canned
   corn
2 tablespoons chopped
   fresh parsley (for
   garnish)

In a large pot, cook the diced bacon lightly to render oil. Add the chopped onion and cook for another 5 minutes, until the onion is softened, but not browned. Add the fish, potatoes, milk, sage, salt, and pepper. Simmer gently (liquid should ripple slightly), stirring occasionally, for about 12 minutes, or until the fish and potatoes are done. Add the canned corn and cook for another 2 minutes.

To serve, pour the chowder into a large tureen or chowder bowl. Garnish with the chopped parsley. Serve with a loaf of fresh home- or bakery-baked white bread cut into thick slices to soak up the sauce.

Serves 6 to 8 generously.

This ideal luncheon dish can be made hours in advance.

Lingcod and Grapefruit Salad

4 cups poached, chilled,
   and flaked lingcod
2 grapefruit
1 cup creamy-style
   commercial onion salad
   dressing
Dash of sugar

1 ½ tablespoons fresh
   grapefruit juice
½ cup finely chopped
   celery
4 teaspoons chopped
   pimiento

Cut the grapefruit in half. Scoop out the fruit, remove all the membrane, and put aside the fruit and juice. Refrigerate the shells.

In a large mixing bowl, combine the salad dressing, grapefruit juice, and sugar. Add the chopped celery, pimiento, and fresh grapefruit sections and toss. Add the fish and gently fold it into the mixture. Stuff the mixture into grapefruit shells and refrigerate until time to eat.

Serves 4.

Red Snapper Amandine

1 ½ pounds red snapper
   fillets
¼ cup lemon juice
2 tablespoons flour

Salt and pepper to taste
4 tablespoons butter
½ cup sliced almonds

Wipe the fish with a damp paper towel. Dip the fish in the lemon juice, then dredge lightly in flour seasoned with salt and pepper. Melt the butter in a frypan and sauté the fish until golden (about 4 to 6 minutes on each side). Remove the fish to a hot serving platter. Add the almonds to the butter in the pan and sauté quickly over medium-high heat. Pour the almonds and the butter over the fish. Serve immediately with lemon wedges.

Serves 4.

Pan-Fried Red Snapper

1 ½ pounds thin red
   snapper fillets
1 egg
¼ cup milk
¼ teaspoon each of salt
   and pepper

½ teaspoon dry mustard
¼ cup grated Parmesan
   cheese
¼ cup bread crumbs
4 tablespoons butter

Beat the egg with the milk, salt, pepper, and mustard in a shallow bowl. Shake the Parmesan cheese and bread crumbs together in a paper bag until well mixed, then spread them on a flat dish or waxed paper. Dip the fillets first in the egg mixture, then roll in the cheese mixture, pressing gently to coat well. Melt the butter in a large frying pan. Sauté the fillets for about 4 minutes on each side, or until the fish flakes easily.

Serves 4.

Baked Snapper Fillets

4 8-ounce red snapper
  fillets
½ lemon
1 teaspoon lemon-pepper
  marinade

1 teaspoon dried parsley
  flakes
1 teaspoon garlic powder
4 strips bacon

Rub the fillets with the cut lemon. Sprinkle both sides of the fish with lemon-pepper, dried parsley, and garlic powder. Wrap each fillet tightly in waxed paper and refrigerate until ready to cook. (Unwrap before cooking.)

Place the fillets in a greased casserole and top with the bacon. Bake at 350 degrees for about 20 minutes, or until fish flakes easily when tested with a fork. Discard the bacon.

Serves 4.

Ginger Snapper

1 ½ pounds red snapper
  fillets
¼ cup gin
½ cup ginger ale

4 medium-size
  gingersnaps, coarsely
  crushed
1 lemon, thinly sliced

Place the fillets in a shallow baking dish. Combine the gin and ginger ale, and pour over the fish. Sprinkle the gingersnap crumbs over the fish and into the liquid. Place the sliced lemon on top of the fish. Cover and bake at 350 degrees for about 20 minutes or until the fish flakes easily.

Serves 4.

Rockfish Wellington

1 rockfish fillet, approximately 12 ounces
11-ounce box piecrust mix

3-ounce package cream cheese
2 teaspoons anchovy paste

Wash the fillet, pat it dry with a paper towel, and set it aside. Follow the directions on the piecrust mix to make 2 crusts. Roll the dough to an oval shape extending 1 inch longer and wider than fillet. In a mixing bowl, soften the cream cheese with the back of a spoon and blend in the anchovy paste. Spread the cream-cheese mixture over the top of the fillet. Place the fillet on one crust. Cover with the second crust. Seal the edges all around by pressing with a fork. Prick the top crust once or twice with a fork. Place the fish in crust on a greased baking sheet and bake at 425 degrees for 22 minutes, then place it under the broiler for 2 to 3 minutes until the crust is golden.

Serves 2.

Fish, pasta, vegetable, and luscious sauce combined! Select your most attractive casserole for an exciting presentation of this delightful dish.

Red Snapper Spinach Pasta

1 ½ pounds thin-sliced
   red snapper fillet,
   poached and boned
1 small package medium
   noodles
1 pint sour cream
10 ¾-ounce can
   condensed cream of
   mushroom soup
¼ teaspoon each of salt

and pepper
¼ cup grated Parmesan
   cheese
2 10-ounce packages
   chopped frozen
   spinach, thawed and
   drained
5-ounce package Swiss
   cheese
Dash of paprika

Cook the noodles as directed on the package. Drain and let cool. In a bowl, mix the sour cream, soup, salt, pepper, and Parmesan cheese. Grease the bottom and sides of a deep 2½-quart ovenproof casserole. Cover the bottom of the casserole with a layer of cooked noodles, then add a layer of spinach. Spoon a thin layer of the sour-cream mixture over the spinach, then place the cooked fish fillets on top of the sour-cream mixture. Add another layer of sour-cream mixture and top with slices of Swiss cheese.

According to the depth of the casserole, repeat with layers of noodles, spinach, and sour-cream mixture, making sure to end up with sour-cream mixture on top. Sprinkle with paprika. Bake at 350 degrees for 1 hour.

Serves 4 to 6.

Red Snapper with Curaçao Sauce

2 pounds red snapper
  fillets

½ lemon
Salt and pepper

Curaçao Sauce:
1 cup sour cream
¾ cup orange juice
¼ cup Curaçao (orange

  liqueur)
3 tablespoons grated
  orange rind

Wipe the fillets with a damp paper towel. Rub the cut lemon all over the fillets. Season with salt and pepper. Place the fillets in a single layer in a lightly greased baking dish. Bake, uncovered, at 350 degrees for 15 minutes.

Meanwhile, make the Curaçao Sauce: In a mixing bowl, combine the sour cream, orange juice, Curaçao, and most of the grated orange rind (reserve some of the rind for garnish). Pour the sauce over the fish and continue baking for approximately 5 minutes, or until the fish flakes easily. Just before serving, sprinkle the remaining orange rind over the fish.

Serves 4 to 5.

Whiskey-Simmered Snapper

8 ounces red snapper
  fillet, cut into bite-size
  pieces
3 tablespoons butter
Dash garlic powder and
  salt

1 large onion, sliced into
  thin rings
¾ teaspoon lemon-
  pepper
2 sprigs fresh parsley
¼ cup favorite whiskey

In a large saucepan, melt the butter and add the garlic powder, salt, and onion rings. Sauté over low heat for about 3 minutes. Add the fish pieces, sprinkle with lemon-pepper, and gently sauté another 4 minutes. Add more butter if necessary. Tear parsley by hand and add it to the pan, stirring constantly. Combine the whiskey and ½ cup water and add it to the pan. Cover and simmer for about 8 minutes.

Serves 2.

Rock and Roll

8 rockfish fillets, ¼ inch
 thick

Rice Medley Stuffing:

1 cup cooked white rice	2 tablespoons soft butter
3 tablespoons chopped	or margarine
black olives	¼ teaspoon salt
3 tablespoons chopped	¼ teaspoon pepper
mushrooms	
2 tablespoons Sauterne	
(or any dry white wine)	

Swiss Cheese Sauce:

2 tablespoons butter or	dry white wine)
margarine	½ cup grated Swiss
2 tablespoons flour	cheese
½ cup half-and-half (half	1 teaspoon dry mustard
milk, half cream)	¼ teaspoon salt
¾ cup Sauterne (or any	¼ teaspoon pepper

Wash the fillets and pat them dry with a paper towel, then set aside. Mix all stuffing ingredients together. If mixture seems loose, add a little more butter. Put a heaping tablespoon of stuffing in the center of each fillet, fold ends over stuffing, and secure with a toothpick. Place fillets in a lightly buttered baking dish, add any leftover stuffing to the dish between the fillets. Bake, uncovered, at 350 degrees for 15 minutes.

Meanwhile, make the Swiss Cheese Sauce: On low

heat, melt the butter in a saucepan and slowly blend in the flour. Add the half-and-half a little at a time, stirring constantly. Then add the wine, still stirring constantly. Add the cheese and stir it until it is completely melted. Remove the saucepan from the heat and add the mustard, salt, and pepper.

Pour the sauce over the rolled fillets and bake for another 5 minutes, or until the fish flakes easily.

Serves 4.

Red Snapper Florentine

4 8-ounce red snapper fillets
2 tablespoons butter
⅓ cup chopped fresh mushrooms
⅓ cup diced celery

⅓ cup diced onion
10-ounce package frozen chopped spinach
2 tablespoons sour cream
Dash each of salt, pepper, garlic powder, and dill

Quick Sour-Cream Sauce:
1 cup sour cream
1 cup dry white wine
1 tablespoon lemon juice
2 teaspoons dillweed

½ teaspoon each of salt, pepper, and dry mustard

Sauté the mushrooms, celery, and onion in butter until soft and golden color, then remove from the heat. Cook the frozen spinach according to the package directions. Drain. In a large mixing bowl, combine ¾ cup of the spinach, the sautéed vegetables, pan drippings, and sour cream. Lightly sprinkle in salt, pepper, garlic powder, and dill. Mix thoroughly.

Wipe the fish with a damp paper towel. Place 2 fillets on a greased baking dish or cookie sheet. Cover each with stuffing, then place the remaining 2 fillets on top. Dot with butter and bake at 350 degrees for about 25 minutes, or until the fish flakes easily when tested with a fork. Accompany with Quick Sour Cream Sauce for your family or guests to pour on top.

To make the sauce: Combine all the ingredients in a saucepan and stir until blended. Place the saucepan on the range over medium heat until sauce is hot, but do not allow to boil. Pour the sauce into a serving bowl and serve at once.

Serves 4 to 6.

Oyster-Stuffed Rockfish

8 medium-size rockfish fillets
2 cups soft bread crumbs
3/4 cup chopped fresh oysters (canned oysters can be substituted)
1 teaspoon minced onion
2 tablespoons lemon juice
2 tablespoons mayonnaise
1 teaspoon salt
1/4 teaspoon pepper

4 tablespoons butter
4 tablespoons flour
1 cup milk
1 cup chicken bouillon
1/2 cup dry white wine (Sauterne)
2 tablespoons grated Parmesan cheese
2 tablespoons minced parsley
Salt and pepper

Place the bread crumbs, oysters, onion, lemon juice, mayonnaise, salt, and pepper in a large bowl. With a fork, mash everything together until the mixture is smooth. Place 4 fillets in a shallow greased baking dish. Spread the oyster filling evenly over each fillet. Arrange the other 4 fillets over the filling.

Melt the butter and blend in the flour. Stir in the milk, bouillon, and wine; cook until thickened, stirring frequently. Stir in the cheese and parsley. Season to taste with salt and pepper.

Pour the sauce over the fillets. Bake in moderate to hot oven (350 to 400 degrees) for 20 minutes, basting occasionally with sauce, or until the fish flakes.

Serves 4.

For a different kind of a party, try a fish fry.

Red Snapper Fish Fry

3 pounds red snapper
fillets, cut into 1-inch
strips
1 ¾ cups packaged biscuit
mix
1 ¼ cups beer
2 eggs, lightly beaten

½ teaspoon salt
¼ teaspoon paprika
1 tablespoon dried
parsley flakes
Cooking oil
Lemon wedges

Place the biscuit mix in a bowl. Slowly stir in the
beer. Add the eggs, salt, paprika, and parsley flakes. Dip
the fish strips into the biscuit batter, coating well. In a
large frypan, pour cooking oil approximately ½ inch
deep. Heat the oil and when it is hot, quickly brown the
fish strips on each side (do not overlap fish). Reduce the
heat slightly and cook for another 5 minutes. Remove
the fish with a wide slotted spatula and drain on a paper
towel. Serve immediately with lots of lemon wedges.

Serves 6 to 8.

Many fish lovers firmly believe that the test of fine fresh fish is how it tastes raw. Raw fish dishes are served all over the world. Sashimi and Sushi are Japanese delicacies. In Mexico, Panama, and other countries of Spanish heritage, the famed chilled raw fish appetizer is known as Ceviche (sometimes spelled Seviche). You can use any fine-textured fish (one or more). We suggest red snapper, abalone, scallops, mahimahi, octopus, and rockfish.

We have found that the delicate fish flavors are best brought out by preparing Ceviche one day in advance.

Ceviche

2 pounds raw fish of your
   choice, diced

Marinade:

6 to 8 large limes (if
   unavailable you can
   substitute lemons;
   however, the same
   flavor is not obtained)
1 1/2 teaspoons salt
1/2 teaspoon tabasco sauce
1 teaspoon sugar

Ceviche Sauce:

2 tomatoes, chopped
1 onion, chopped
4 small chile peppers,
   seeded and chopped
   (or 1/2 green pepper,
   seeded and chopped)
1 teaspoon chopped
cilantro
1/3 cup olive oil
2 tablespoons wine
   vinegar
1 avocado, sliced
   (optional)

In a large bowl, mix the lime juice, salt, tabasco sauce, and sugar. Add the diced fish, stir gently, cover and marinate in the refrigerator for at least 5 hours.

Drain and toss the fish in a sauce made of the tomatoes, onion, chiles or green pepper, cilantro, oil, and vinegar. Chill thoroughly before serving. Serve in small bowls or cocktail glasses as an appetizer. Garnish with sliced avocado, if desired.

Serves 8.

Tomato-Broiled Sea Bass

1 sea bass fillet,
  approximately 13
  ounces
¼ lemon
1 tomato, cut into ⅛-

inch-thick slices
2 strips bacon
Garlic powder and
  pepper to taste

Rinse the fillet briefly under cold water, then pat dry with a paper towel. Rub the fillet with the lemon wedge. Place the fish in a greased baking pan and sprinkle with garlic powder. Cover the fish with tomato slices and top with bacon. Sprinkle with pepper and broil for approximately 10 minutes, or until the fish flakes easily when tested with a fork.

Serves 2.

Fillet à la Frank

1 ½-pound sea bass fillet
Salt, pepper, and paprika
  to taste
4 tablespoons melted

butter
1 whole shallot bulb,
  minced
⅓ cup dry white wine

Wipe the fish with a damp paper towel and pat dry. Sprinkle with salt, pepper, and paprika. Add the shallot to the melted butter and stir. Pour it into a shallow baking pan. Place the fish in the butter-shallot mixture, turning to coat both sides. Pour the wine over the fish. Baste the fish before placing the pan under the broiler. Broil for approximately 12 minutes, basting occasionally, until the fish flakes easily.

Serves 4.

Bass in Baskets

4 sea bass fillets,
     approximately 8 ounces
     each
½ cup mayonnaise
1 cup sour cream
2 tablespoons melted
     butter

½ pound mushrooms,
     sliced and sautéed
½ pound small seedless
     green grapes
Salt and pepper to taste
½ lemon
Paprika

Mix together the mayonnaise, sour cream, butter, mushrooms, and grapes. Season with salt and pepper and set aside.

Make 4 individual aluminum-foil baskets and place a fillet in each. Season with a squeeze of lemon juice. Spoon sour-cream mixture over each and bake in a 350-degree oven for 20 minutes, or until the fish passes the fork test. Broil for 1 minute to brown slightly. Sprinkle with paprika and serve right in the foil baskets.

Serves 4.

Poached Bass with Rémoulade Sauce

4 bass fillets
Basic Poaching Liquid
     (*see* page 104)

2 sprigs parsley, chopped

Rémoulade Sauce:
1 cup mayonnaise
2 tablespoons chopped
     cucumber
2 tablespoons chopped

parsley
1 tablespoon anchovy
     paste
1 tablespoon capers

Follow the Basic Fish Poaching recipe to prepare the bass fillets. Carefully remove the fish from the poaching liquid and place it on a hot platter. Sprinkle with parsley and serve with the sauce.

Rémoulade Sauce is easily made by combining all the sauce ingredients in a mixing bowl. Chill before serving.

Serves 4.

This hearty, colorful dish is a real man-pleaser!

Skillet Sea Bass

2 pounds sea bass fillet
4 tablespoons cooking oil
¼ teaspoon each of salt, pepper, and garlic powder
1 onion, diced in large chunks
1 green pepper, cut into large pieces

1 tablespoon commercial chili sauce
10¼-ounce can marinara sauce
½ cup dry Sauterne wine
1 tomato, cut into wedges
3 large pitted black olives, sliced

Pour the oil in a large heavy skillet and add salt, pepper, and garlic powder. Slowly sauté the onion and green pepper until soft but not dark.

In a small bowl, combine the chili sauce with marinara sauce and add it to the ingredients in the skillet. Add the wine and stir.

Put the fish in the skillet and add the tomato and black olives. Spoon the entire sauce mixture completely over the fish. Cover the skillet and cook over low heat for 20 minutes. Remove the lid and cook for another 5 minutes, or until the fish flakes easily.

Serves 4 to 6.

Sea Bass Casserole

¾ pound sea bass fillet, cut into 2-inch cubes (be sure all bones are removed)
10-ounce package frozen chopped broccoli
10½-ounce can condensed cream of shrimp soup
¼ cup heavy cream
½ cup Chablis (or other dry white wine)
3 tablespoons melted butter
½ cup cooked baby shrimp

Defrost the broccoli and drain until all the liquid is out. In a mixing bowl, combine the soup with the heavy cream and wine, mix thoroughly, and set aside. Spread the melted butter inside a deep casserole. Put the broccoli in the casserole and mix with the butter. Sprinkle the shrimp over the broccoli. Add the fish cubes, covering the shrimp. Pour the soup mixture over the fish cubes. Cover the casserole and bake at 350 degrees for 20 minutes. Remove the cover and bake for another 10 minutes, or until the fish flakes easily.

Serves 4.

Sea Bass Barbecue

2 pounds sea bass fillets

Tomato-Sherry Marinade:
1 onion, chopped
½ clove garlic, finely chopped
½ cup melted butter
8-ounce can tomato sauce
¼ cup sherry
½ teaspoon sugar
1 teaspoon Worcestershire sauce
Pinch each of oregano, thyme, salt, and pepper

Wash the fillets in cold, salted water. Dry them with a paper towel and set aside. Sauté the onion and garlic in the melted butter until tender. Add the remaining marinade ingredients, stir, and allow to cool. Place the fillets in the Tomato-Sherry Marinade and refrigerate for 30 minutes. Then remove the fillets from the marinade and arrange in a hinged, well-greased wire grill. Barbecue over very hot coals for 4 to 7 minutes per side, basting often with the marinade.

Another excellent marinade for sea bass features soy sauce and cognac: In a large mixing bowl, combine ½ cup melted butter, the juice of 1 lemon, 2 tablespoons soy sauce, a dash of garlic powder, and ½ cup cognac. Marinate the fillets and barbecue according to the above instructions.

Serves 4.

Sea Bass with Yogurt Sauce

2 pounds sea bass fillets (or steaks)
½ pound fresh mushrooms
2 tablespoons butter
1 tablespoon cooking oil
½ teaspoon salt
½ teaspoon pepper
¼ cup dry white wine
1 cup plain yogurt
½ cup half-and-half (half milk, half cream)
¼ cup lemon juice
¼ teaspoon paprika
½ teaspoon dry mustard
¼ pound cooked baby shrimp (optional)
2 tablespoons chopped fresh parsley

Wash the mushrooms and remove the hard end of each stem. Cut the mushrooms into slices about ¼ inch thick. Melt the butter in a large baking dish and add the oil. Sauté the mushrooms in the baking dish on the top of the stove over medium heat for 3 to 4 minutes. Sprinkle with salt and pepper, add the wine, and cook for another 3 to 4 minutes. Meanwhile, in a mixing bowl, combine the yogurt, half-and-half, lemon juice, paprika, dry mustard, and baby shrimp (reserve a few shrimp for garnish).

Remove the baking dish from the heat, push the mushrooms to the side, and place the fish in center of dish. Pour the yogurt sauce over the fish, and sprinkle with parsley. Bake, uncovered, at 400 degrees for about 20 minutes, or until the fish flakes easily. Garnish with the remaining cooked shrimp or thinly sliced lemon.

Serves 4 to 6.

This elegant dish is guaranteed to win raves from your guests. The crêpes can be made that morning, or even the day before, and refrigerated until needed. Just be sure each crêpe is separated by a sheet of waxed paper, and cover the entire stack of crêpes with additional waxed paper to keep them from drying out. The fish may also be poached that morning or the day before and refrigerated until needed. Do not flake the fish until you are ready to prepare the recipe, otherwise it will become too dry. Halibut, lingcod, or rockfish may be substituted for sea bass. Bon appetit!

Crêpes Stuffed with Sea Bass

2 cups (1 pound) flaked and boned poached sea bass
10¾-ounce can condensed cream of celery soup
¼ cup poaching liquid
¼ cup heavy cream
3 tablespoons chopped mushrooms (canned)

2 tablespoons chopped pimiento
¼ teaspoon salt
¼ teaspoon pepper
½ cup sherry
2 tablespoons melted butter
2 ounces Grand Marnier to flame crêpes (optional)

Crêpes:
2 eggs
¾ teaspoon salt

¾ cup flour
Cooking oil to grease pan

First, make your crêpes: Break the eggs into a bowl and beat thoroughly. Mix the salt into the flour and add slowly to the beaten eggs, stirring until smooth. Slowly add 1 cup water and stir thoroughly. Pour a small amount of cooking oil into a heavy 5-inch frypan and spread the oil evenly with a paper towel. Heat the pan. For easier handling, dip a cup into the batter and pour a scant measure into the hot pan, tilting pan as you pour so that batter spreads evenly over the entire bottom surface. When the edges of the crêpe start to curl away from pan (within 1 minute or so), lift it gently with your fingers and flip it over to cook it on the other side (about 1 minute). Turn the crêpe onto a plate. If the pan is dry, lightly grease it again for the next crêpe. Place a sheet of waxed paper between each crêpe as you stack them. This recipe makes 8 to 10 crêpes.

To stuff crêpes: In a mixing bowl, combine the soup, poaching liquid, heavy cream, mushrooms, pimiento, salt, pepper, and ¼ cup of the sherry. This will make 2 cups of sauce. Reserve 1 cup and set it aside. Mix the remaining cup of sauce with the flaked fish. Put 2 tablespoons of stuffing mixture on each crêpe and then roll up the crêpe over the mixture.

Spread melted butter in your prettiest large, shallow baking dish. Place a single layer of stuffed crêpes in the dish. Add the remaining sherry to the reserved cup of sauce, and pour in a strip across the center of the crêpes. Bake, uncovered, at 350 degrees for 15 minutes. When ready to serve, pour Grand Marnier over the crêpes, and flame with long taper match.

Serves 4 or 5.

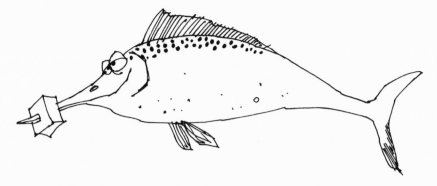

Swordfish is firm-textured and tastes somewhat like white veal or chicken. This meunière *preparation enhances its delicate flavor.*

Swordfish Steak Meunière

1 ½ pounds swordfish
  steak, ¾ inch thick
½ cup milk (to marinate
  fish)
Dash each of salt, pepper,
  paprika, and dry
  mustard

3 tablespoons butter
½ medium onion, diced
2 tablespoons lemon
  juice
¼ cup salted roasted
  sunflower seeds
  (optional)

    Pour the milk into a shallow dish. Lay the swordfish steak in the milk, cover the dish, and refrigerate for ½ hour, turning the fish once.

    Remove the fish from the milk and discard the milk. Sprinkle the fish with salt, pepper, paprika, and dry mustard on both sides. Slowly melt the butter in a baking dish. Dip the fish in the butter, turning to coat both sides. Add the diced onion to the melted butter welling around fish. Sprinkle with the lemon juice. Bake, uncovered, at 350 degrees for about 20 minutes, or until the fish flakes easily. Remove the fish to a heated serving platter, pour the butter with onions over the top. Garnish with sunflower seeds and serve immediately.

Serves 4.

Broiled Swordfish Steak

1 swordfish steak,
approximately 12 to 14
ounces

½ cup commercial Italian
dressing
Paprika

Pour the dressing in a shallow bowl. Place the fish in the dressing and marinate for 1 hour in the refrigerator, turning once.

Remove the fish from the marinade and reserve ¼ cup of the marinade. Place the fish in a broiler pan and sprinkle with paprika. Pour the reserved marinade over the fish. Broil for about 8 minutes, or until the fish flakes easily.

Serves 2.

Betty's Favorite Swordfish

2 pounds swordfish steak,
approximately ¾ inch
thick
¾ cup butter

Juice of 2 lemons
1 tablespoon garlic
powder

Wipe the fish with a damp paper towel and pat dry. Melt the butter, add the lemon juice and garlic powder, and stir until blended. Generously brush the butter baste on both sides of the fish. Place the steaks on a greased barbecue grill. Barbecue for 4 minutes per side, basting often.

Serves 4.

Spanish Swordfish

1½ pounds swordfish
steak, ¾ inch thick
1 tablespoon basil
6 tablespoons butter
1 lemon
1 teaspoon olive juice

(from jar of olives)
8 pimiento-stuffed
Spanish olives, thinly
sliced

Rub the swordfish with basil. Melt the butter, remove it from the heat, and add the juice of 1 lemon and the olive juice. Lay the fish in a baking dish and heavily brush it with the butter baste. Cover the fish with the sliced olives and brush again with the baste. Bake in a 350-degree oven, occasionally brushing with the baste, for 20 minutes.

Serves 4.

Swordfish in Horseradish Sauce

1½ pounds swordfish
steak, ¾ inch thick
1 cup sour cream
3 tablespoons milk
1 tablespoon cream-style
white horseradish
2 tablespoons lemon
juice

1 teaspoon capers (with
juice)
1 teaspoon dry mustard
2 tablespoons fresh
chopped parsley
Salt and pepper to taste
3 tablespoons butter

First, prepare the sauce by combining the sour cream, milk, horseradish, lemon juice, capers, dry mustard, and parsley.

Sprinkle the swordfish steak with salt and pepper. Melt the butter in a baking dish and turn the fish over in the butter to coat both sides. Pour the sauce over the fish. Bake, uncovered, at 350 degrees for 25 minutes, or until the fish flakes easily. Garnish with additional chopped parsley and thinly sliced lemon.

Serves 4.

This gourmet dish is unbelievably easy to make and tastes as though you slaved over it for hours.

Swordfish in Pastry

¾-pound swordfish steak, ¾ inch thick
11-ounce box piecrust mix

3-ounce package cream cheese
2 teaspoons onion soup mix

Wipe the fish with a damp paper towel and pat it dry. Remove the skin from around the edge of the steak. Follow the directions on the piecrust mix to make 2 crusts. Roll the crusts to the shape of the fish, extending them approximately 1 inch longer all around.

In a mixing bowl, soften the cream cheese with the back of a spoon and blend in the onion soup mix. Spread the cream-cheese mixture over the top of the fish. Place the fish on one crust and cover with the second crust. Seal the edges all around by pressing with a fork. Prick the top crust once or twice with the fork. Place the fish in pastry on a greased baking sheet. Bake at 425 degrees for 22 minutes and then place under the broiler for approximately 2 minutes until the crust is golden.

Serves 2.

Swordfish in Zesty Cheese Sauce

1 1/2 pounds swordfish
   steak
3/4 cup milk
1/4 teaspoon salt
1/4 teaspoon pepper
2 tablespoons butter

1/4 cup Chablis wine
2 tablespoons lemon
   juice
Chopped spinach or
   chopped broccoli
   (optional)

Zesty Cheese Sauce:
2 tablespoons butter
2 tablespoons flour
1/2 cup milk (from
   marinade)
1/4 cup heavy cream
1/2 cup Chablis wine

2/3 cup grated sharp
   Cheddar cheese
1 teaspoon
   Worcestershire sauce
Salt and pepper to taste

Pour the milk into a shallow dish. Lay the swordfish steak in the milk and cover the dish. Refrigerate the fish for 1/2 hour, turning once. Remove the fish from the milk and reserve 1/2 cup of the milk for the sauce. Season the fish with salt and pepper. Melt the butter in a baking dish. Lay the fish in the butter and turn it to coat both sides. Pour the wine and lemon juice over the fish. Bake, uncovered, at 350 degrees for 15 minutes.

Meanwhile, make the sauce: On low heat, melt the butter in a saucepan and slowly blend in the flour. Add the milk and cream a little at a time, stirring constantly. Add the wine and continue stirring. Add the cheese and stir until it is completely melted. Remove the saucepan from the heat, stir in the Worcestershire sauce, salt, and pepper.

Pour the sauce over swordfish and bake for another 5 minutes, or until the fish flakes easily. Serve on top of cooked chopped spinach or cooked chopped broccoli for an extra delicious touch.

Serves 4.

Here's an excellent luncheon dish, using leftover cooked fish.

Swordfish-Stuffed Tomatoes

1¼ cups flaked cooked
  swordfish (remove any
  skin or bones)
4 large unpeeled
  tomatoes
⅓ cup sour cream
2 tablespoons creamed
  white horseradish sauce

1 tablespoon finely diced
  onion
1 teaspoon capers (with
  juice)
1 teaspoon dillweed
Salt and pepper to taste
1 tablespoon cooking oil

Wash the tomatoes and wipe dry. With a sharp-pointed knife or serrated grapefruit knife, cut into the top of each tomato, hollowing out a deep cavity for the stuffing (do not break through the skin). Remove the seeds and pulp. Turn the tomatoes upside down on a paper towel for 10 minutes, so that the excess juice will drain out.

Combine the sour cream, horseradish, onion, capers, dillweed, salt, and pepper in a mixing bowl. Add the swordfish, mixing gently in order to keep the fish from mashing. Spread the cooking oil in a baking dish with a paper towel. Use the excess oil on the paper towel to wipe over the outside of the tomatoes. Sprinkle salt inside the tomatoes, then spoon in the stuffing mixture. Place the tomatoes, stuffing-side up, in a baking dish. (If the tomatoes won't stand upright in the baking dish, place them in a well-greased muffin pan.) Bake at 350 degrees for 20 to 25 minutes, until the tomatoes are done.

Serves 4.

TIPS ON BONING DRESSED TROUT

You may wish to bone dressed trout prior to stuffing and cooking. This way, when your trout is prepared and ready for serving, your family and guests can dine without fear of swallowing the bones.

It is important to the appearance of your entrée to keep the head and tail attached to the trout. Lay the fish on a flat surface, open the body cavity (which has previously been gutted), and insert a sharp knife under the backbone at the head. Carefully cut between the ribs and the flesh. Do not cut through the back of the fish and break the skin. Release the bones from the back of the fish. Repeat the operation on the other side of the trout. You should then be able to remove the whole bone structure in one piece. Discard.

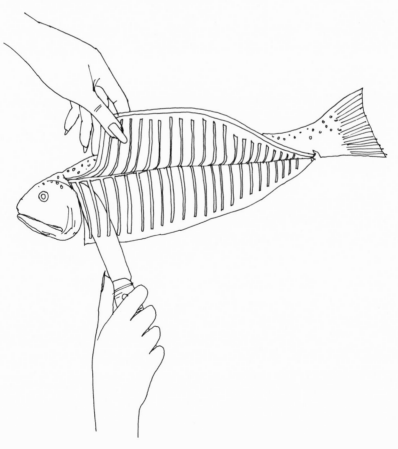

Citrus-Barbecued Trout

1 trout per serving,
  cleaned
Butter

Salt and pepper
Lemons, limes
Onion

Rub the whole trout with butter and sprinkle with salt and pepper. Cut a small wedge of lemon and onion for each trout and insert them into each open cavity. Tear heavy-duty aluminum foil into individual large squares. Place each trout on a separate piece of foil. Squeeze ½ lemon and ½ lime on each trout. Wrap foil tightly around the trout. Place the packages on the grill. Barbecue over fairly hot coals for 20 minutes. There is no need to turn the fish.

For an extra garnish you may wish to add sliced mushrooms or almonds prior to barbecuing. If so, turn trout packages once while on the grill so that the mushrooms or nuts do not stick to the foil.

Clam-and-Shrimp-Stuffed Trout

6 trout
1/2 pound mushrooms, sliced
1 onion, minced
Olive oil
2 cups sour cream
2 small cans clams
2 small cans shrimp

1 medium bell pepper, finely shredded
1/2 teaspoon allspice
1/2 teaspoon paprika
1/4 teaspoon coarse ground pepper
2 lemons

Sauté the mushrooms and onion in olive oil. In a separate bowl, combine the sour cream, clams, shrimp, bell pepper, and spices. Add the sautéed mushrooms and onion. Place each trout on an individual piece of oiled heavy-duty aluminum foil. Stuff each fish with some clam-shrimp mixture. Sprinkle with the juice of the lemons. Pour any remaining liquid on top of the fish. Carefully wrap and seal each package. Bake at 325 degrees for about 30 minutes.

Serves 6.

Camping out? There's nothing like fresh trout for breakfast. Here's a different way to prepare your early morning catch.

Breakfast Trout Patties

Trout, cleaned, skinned, and boned
Egg
Salt, pepper, and garlic

powder
Seasoned cracker crumbs or seasoned flour
Butter

In a large bowl, break up the trout with a fork. Break in the egg. Season with salt, pepper, and garlic powder and mix thoroughly. By hand, make patties (similar to the way you would make hamburger patties). Coat the patties evenly with crumbs or flour and sauté in butter in a pan over hot camp coals for about 3 minutes per side.

Fresh-Caught Trout Cookout

Trout, cleaned	Pepper
Cold salt-water solution	Flour (optional)
Lemons	Butter

In a large pot, make a salt-water solution (approximately 2 tablespoons salt per quart of cold water) and set aside. Pierce a hole on both sides of fish behind the head area. Soak fish in the salt-water brine—small fish for 1 hour, longer for larger fish. Every few minutes, massage the fish (rub the brine into them).

After soaking, wipe the fish but do not wash them. Squeeze lemon juice over the fish and season with pepper. If the trout are small, sprinkle them with enough flour to prevent them from sticking to the pan; otherwise, no flour is necessary. Melt the butter in the pan and add the trout when the pan is very hot. Cook for 7 minutes (for medium-size fish), shaking the pan constantly. Turn the fish over. Cover and cook for another 8 to 10 minutes, still shaking the pan constantly. The small holes in the fish will permit the heat to evenly cook the upper, thicker portion. This process of steam cooking will also allow for easy removal of the bones.

Truite au bleu, *respected as the national fish dish of Switzerland, is superlative. In order to cook a trout so that it turns blue, it is imperative to kill the fish only seconds before preparing. In this case, have your husband bring his catch home alive.*

After a knockout blow on the head, clean the fish immediately and run them quickly under cold water. Not too much water should be used or the outer film causing the blue phenomenon will be washed away. Immediately start cooking the trout according to the following recipe.

Swiss au Bleu

4 medium trout, cleaned
2 quarts salted water
½ cup dry white wine
   or 1 cup cider or mild
   vinegar
2 bay leaves

1 medium onion, sliced
1 medium carrot, sliced
3 large sprigs of parsley
8 peppercorns
1 stalk celery, cut into
   chunks

Prepare a court-bouillon by combining all the ingredients except the trout in a large pot. Bring to a boil, reduce the heat to a simmer, cover, and cook for another 15 minutes. Strain out the vegetables. Plunge the trout into the bouillon. The fish should turn blue immediately. Cover the pot and continue cooking at a low simmer for 5 to 10 minutes, or until the trout are done (when eyes pop). NOTE: Court-bouillon may be prepared in advance and kept for weeks before using.

Drain the fish and serve on a dish lined with a linen napkin (to absorb the excess moisture and keep the fish

firm and warm). The classical manner of displaying blue
trout is to bend the fish into a U-shape.

Serves 4.

Many other countries boast similar trout recipes.
Substituting 1 dried red chile, 1 raw jalapeño, 1 clove
garlic, crushed, and 1 large pinch of tomillio (thyme) for
the bay leaves, peppercorns, and parsley of the Swiss
bouillon will provide a Mexican *truchas azul* entrée.

Trout de Verde

3 trout, cleaned and
  boned
1/4 pound fresh
  mushrooms, sliced
4 scallions, sliced
Salt, pepper, and
  garlic powder to
  taste
4 tablespoons melted
  butter
1 cup sherry
1 stalk celery, chopped

6 ounces cooked bay
  shrimp (if fresh
  unavailable,
  substitute canned)
3 tablespoons
  mayonnaise
1/2 cup seasoned bread
  crumbs
1/4 cup Parmesan cheese
8-ounce can seedless
  grapes (save liquid)

Sauté the mushrooms and scallions in 1 tablespoon
butter with salt, pepper, and garlic powder for 3 minutes.
Add 1/4 cup of the sherry, cover, and simmer over a low
flame for 10 minutes. Uncover the frypan, add the celery,
and simmer for another 2 minutes. Remove the pan from
the heat. Place the mixture in a bowl. Add the shrimp,
mayonnaise, bread crumbs, and cheese. Stir.

Wash the fish and pat them dry with a paper towel.
Season with salt and pepper. Stuff each fish with a third
of the shrimp mixture. Place the fish in a shallow, well-

buttered baking dish. Make two or three shallow cuts on top of each fish. Bake, uncovered, at 400 degrees for 10 minutes. Brush the fish with 3 tablespoons of the melted butter. Add the remaining sherry and the grapes with their liquid. Continue to bake, uncovered, for about 15 minutes. The trout is done when it flakes easily with a fork. Also, the eyes pop when the fish is cooked.

Serves 3.

One of the most beautiful buffet presentations is cold trout in aspic. Decorated with truffles, pimiento, scallion stems, and eggs in a gelatin, it can display a spring flower personality. You certainly must have seen this dish at many restaurants and you might have wondered how you, too, could prepare it at home. The ingredients are simple to purchase.

Cold Trout in Aspic

3 trout, cleaned
3 cups clam juice
2 tablespoons white wine
  vinegar
1 envelope unflavored
  gelatin
Scallions (green onion

stems)
Hard-boiled egg
  whites, sliced thin
1 can black truffles,
  sliced
1 small jar pimiento

Combine the clam juice and vinegar in a pot and bring to a boil. Add the trout and cover the pot. Simmer for 6 minutes, or until the fish flakes easily when tested with a fork. Remove the trout and reserve the cooking bouillon.

To make the aspic: Soften the gelatin in ½ cup cold water and dissolve in 1½ cups of the reserved hot fish bouillon. Let the gelatin cool until it reaches the consistency of raw egg white.

Meanwhile, place the trout on a wire rack and set the rack over a dish. Make two diagonal cuts on one side of each fish, a few inches apart. Pry under the incisions to loosen the skin, then peel off the skin with your fingers, leaving the heads and tails intact.

Spoon a layer of aspic over each fish and refrigerate until the aspic is set.

Make a flower design by trimming green parts of scallions as the stems. Cut the egg white slices to look like petals. Use truffles and pimiento strips as the flower-buds. Dip these decorations in aspic and arrange on each fish. Chill. Cover with layers of aspic, chilling after each layer is applied.

To serve, place the trout on a large platter, garnish with chopped apple and serve with mayonnaise.

Serves 3.

This should be made in advance to allow marinade to penetrate fish.

Trout Antipasto

A 4-pound trout, cleaned
1 medium onion, chopped
4 tablespoons olive oil
2 bay leaves
6 whole cloves
1 stalk celery, chopped
1 medium green pepper, chopped
3 carrots, sliced thin
8 pimiento-stuffed green olives, sliced
2 cups canned peeled tomatoes (with liquid)
1 tablespoon finely chopped parsley
2 tablespoons capers
1 teaspoon salt
1 teaspoon sugar
½ teaspoon pepper
1 clove garlic, crushed

Sauté the onion in 2 tablespoons olive oil until softened. Tie the bay leaves and cloves in a piece of cheesecloth. Add all the ingredients except the trout to sautéed onions. Simmer for about 15 minutes.

Meanwhile, prepare freshly caught trout by placing the fish in a large pan. Pour boiling water slowly over the fish. Remove the head, fins, and skin (it will peel off easily). Carefully bone and cut fish into bite-size pieces. Season and sauté the trout pieces lightly in 2 tablespoons additional oil until golden-brown.

Add the fish to the vegetables. Simmer until the carrots are soft. Discard the bag of herbs. Spoon the mixture into a bowl and refrigerate overnight. Serve as an appetizer with assorted Italian vegetables and sausages.

Trout Party Dip

4 medium-size frozen
  trout

Boiling Liquid:
3 bay leaves
2 teaspoons dried parsley
  flakes
4 tablespoons butter

½ teaspoon pepper
Juice of ½ lemon
2 teaspoons salt

Cocktail Sauce:
¼ cup horseradish
¼ cup lemon juice
1 cup catsup

Take the trout out of the freezer and run hot water over them. Cut off the heads. Go along the backbones with a sharp knife and split the skin. With pliers, pull off the skin. The meat should remain intact since fish are still frozen.

Take a 2-quart-size kettle (not larger, so that you will be able to crowd the pan with the fish) and add just enough water to cover the fish, but do not add the fish. Put the Boiling Liquid ingredients into the water and bring to a boil, stirring to get a nice mixture and aroma. Drop in the fish.

Cook for 6 to 8 minutes, depending upon the thickness of the trout. Check carefully. As soon as the trout are tender, take them out of the pot and open them up. All the bones should come out intact.

Break up the fish with a fork. Any remaining bones can be easily picked out. Mix the fish in a bowl with ¼ cup of the cooking liquid.

In a separate bowl, combine the Cocktail Sauce ingredients. The fish and cocktail sauce can be combined together in one bowl or served in separate bowls. This dish will keep beautifully for 10 days in the refrigerator.

Serves 8 to 10.

Trout Tempter Hors d'Oeuvre

2 medium trout	1/2 teaspoon salt
1 large bay leaf	2 cups vinegar
10 peppercorns	1 medium onion, sliced
8 juniper berries	into thin rings
(optional)	1/2 teaspoon dillweed

Cover the trout with cold water and add the bay leaf, peppercorns, salt, and berries. Boil gently for about 2 minutes, or until the fish is soft. Drain the fish, bone and skin, and set aside.

In a second pot, bring the vinegar and sliced onion to a gentle boil. Cook until the onion rings are wilted.

Place the trout in a shallow dish and cover with the hot vinegar and onion. Sprinkle with dillweed and refrigerate at least overnight. Serve chilled in the marinade.

And Other Wild Games:

Rabbit and Venison

Rabbit is a delicious, tasty meat, similar in flavor to chicken. We generally found most rabbit to be quite tender; however, if you are uncertain of the age of your rabbit, you can tenderize it by marinating. Marinades not only serve to tenderize but also to enhance the flavor of the meat as part of the food preparation.

Fried Rabbit

2 rabbits, cut up
Salt, pepper, and garlic
  powder
2 eggs

½ cup flour
¾ cup bread crumbs
Cooking oil

Add the spices to the eggs and 2 tablespoons water and beat lightly. Dip the rabbit pieces into the egg mixture, then into the flour. Dip the pieces into the egg mixture again, then into the bread crumbs. Sprinkle the coated pieces with a little more of the spices. Place the rabbit pieces on a platter, cover and refrigerate until ½ hour before cooking (to "set" the crust), then allow the rabbit to come to room temperature.

Pour cooking oil to ¼ inch depth in a large frypan. Brown the rabbit pieces on both sides in the oil until golden color. Pour ½ cup water into the pan and immediately cover it with a lid. Reduce the heat to a low simmer. Cook the rabbit for 25 minutes. Remove the cover and cook for another 10 minutes to crisp the crust. Serve the rabbit on a platter garnished with jellied cranberry sauce.

Serves 4 to 6.

Crunchy Coated Rabbit

A 2½-pound rabbit, cut
  up
½ cup evaporated milk
1 cup crushed cornflake
  crumbs
1 teaspoon salt

⅛ teaspoon pepper
¼ teaspoon garlic
  powder
1 teaspoon paprika
Butter

Wash the rabbit pieces and dry them thoroughly. Soak the pieces in evaporated milk for 30 minutes. Into a paper or plastic bag, pour the cornflake crumbs, salt, garlic powder, and pepper. Drop one rabbit piece at a time into the bag, shake well, then remove and place meat-side up on a shallow baking pan. Do not crowd the pan. Sprinkle with paprika and dot with butter. Bake at 350 degrees for 1 hour, or until tender.

Serves 2 to 3.

This is a traditional style of preparing rabbit. The spicy sauce is similar to a Sauerbraten.

Hasenpfeffer

2 rabbits, cut up
  (approximately 4
  pounds)

Hasenpfeffer Marinade:
1 1/2 cups vinegar
1 cup dry red wine
2 onions, sliced
1 shallot bulb, sliced
2 bay leaves
6 whole cloves

1/4 cup flour
1/3 cup bacon drippings
3/4 cup red-currant jelly

1 teaspoon each of salt,
  pepper, and dry
  mustard
1 tablespoon thyme
Pinch of mace

Combine all the marinade ingredients with 1 1/2 cups water in a large bowl. Place the rabbit in the marinade. Cover and refrigerate for 24 hours, turning the meat in the marinade once or twice.

Remove the rabbit from the marinade and dry the pieces with a paper towel. Strain and save the marinade;

also reserve 1 cup of onions from the marinade. Dredge the rabbit lightly in the flour and reserve the remaining flour. Pour the bacon drippings into a large skillet and brown the rabbit pieces on both sides. Remove the rabbit to an ovenproof casserole with a tight-fitting lid (or to a Dutch oven). Sauté the onions reserved from the marinade in the bacon drippings. When the onions are golden, remove them with a slotted spoon (to drain the grease) and add them to the rabbit in the casserole. Pour off the bacon drippings remaining in the skillet. Add the strained marinade to the skillet. Soften the jelly by stirring with a spoon, mix into marinade. Bring to a boil, then reduce the heat. Add enough water to the reserved flour to make a paste. Slowly stir the flour paste into the marinade mixture until the sauce reaches the desired thickness. Pour the sauce over the rabbit. Cover the casserole and place it in a 350-degree oven for about 1½ hours, or until the rabbit is tender. Serve with buttered noodles.

Serves 4 to 6.

Pork-Stuffed Roast Rabbit

1 whole rabbit, cleaned (approximately 3 pounds)
Salt, pepper, and garlic powder

2 tablespoons flour
4 tablespoons butter (for cheesecloth)
Extra butter for baste

Sausage Stuffing:
½ cup pork sausage
4 tablespoons butter
1 onion, coarsely diced
⅓ cup diced celery

1½ cups dried bread cubes
3 tablespoons chopped black olives

First make your stuffing. Break the sausage into small chunks and heat it in a skillet until it is lightly browned. Remove the chunks of sausage and set them aside. Add the butter to the sausage drippings. Sauté the onion and celery until soft; push them to the side of the pan. Add the bread cubes and stir until the cubes have absorbed all the pan drippings. Stir all the ingredients together. Remove the pan from the heat. Stir in the browned sausage chunks and the black olives. Set the stuffing aside to cool slightly while preparing the rabbit. Also, at this time, preheat the oven to 350 degrees.

Wash the rabbit inside and out and pat it dry with a paper towel. Sprinkle it inside and out with salt, pepper, and garlic powder. Lightly dust the outside of the rabbit with flour.

Spoon the stuffing into the cavity, then sew it closed. Melt the butter and soak a length of cheesecloth (large enough to cover the entire rabbit) in the melted butter. Wrap the rabbit completely in cheesecloth, taking care not to pull the cloth too tight, otherwise it will stick to the meat while roasting. Place the rabbit on its side on a rack in the roasting pan. Place the pan in the oven, uncovered, and roast for 40 minutes, checking occasionally to see that the cheesecloth has sufficient butter baste. If the cheesecloth appears dry, add more butter. Turn the rabbit on its other side and continue roasting for about 40 minutes, or until tender. If rabbit is not sufficiently browned, remove the cheesecloth, baste the rabbit, and roast for another 3 to 4 minutes. Serve with cranberry sauce or escalloped apples.

To make pan gravy: Stir 1 cup hot chicken bouillon into the pan drippings, add flour to thicken, and season to taste.

Serves 4 to 5.

Hamilton's Hare

2 rabbits, cut up
½ cup white wine (or dry sherry)
¼ cup red wine (preferably Burgundy)
½ cup olive oil
1 teaspoon each of tarragon, Beau Monde,
and salt
1 clove garlic, minced
2 tablespoons chopped fresh parsley
½ teaspoon chopped chives
Dash of pepper

Combine all the ingredients (except the rabbit) in a large bowl or pot. Soak the rabbit in the marinade for 2 hours or longer. Barbecue the rabbit on a greased grill over very hot coals for approximately 45 minutes. While barbecuing, baste with the remaining marinade.

Serves 4 to 6.

Mole is a traditional Mexican dish featuring peanuts, chocolate, and chile. The sauce is often used for chicken.

Rabbit Mole

A 2½-pound rabbit, cut up
⅛ cup oil
1 clove garlic, minced
1 medium onion, chopped
1 canned green chile, chopped
1 large tomato, peeled and diced
5 teaspoons chili powder
1 ounce unsweetened chocolate, grated
1 tablespoon sesame seeds
Grated peel of ½ small orange
¼ cup peanut butter
½ banana, chopped
Dash of cloves and nutmeg
Salt and pepper

Simmer the rabbit pieces in salted water to cover until tender. Drain and set aside, reserving 2½ cups of the broth. (If you do not have enough broth left over, add chicken broth.) Heat the oil in a skillet and add the garlic, onion, chile, tomato, and chili powder. Cook until the onion is tender but not brown. Add the broth and bring to a boil. Add the grated chocolate, sesame seeds, orange peel, peanut butter, banana, cloves, and nutmeg. Blend the sauce until it is smooth. Simmer, uncovered, for 30 minutes, or until slightly thickened. If the sauce becomes too thick, add additional broth. Add the rabbit pieces and salt and pepper to taste. Cover and simmer for 10 minutes.

Serves 2 to 3.

Creamed Rabbit with Mushrooms

2 rabbits, cut up
½ cup flour seasoned
   with ½ teaspoon
   pepper
6 tablespoons butter
¼ cup diced onions
8 large fresh mushrooms,
   sliced

1½ tablespoons onion
   soup mix
⅔ cup hot chicken
   bouillon
1½ cups sour cream

Dredge the rabbit pieces in flour. Place half the butter in a large frypan and add the onions. Sauté the onions until soft. Push the onions to side of the frypan and brown the rabbit pieces on both sides.

Meanwhile, put the other 3 tablespoons of butter in a separate frypan and sauté the mushrooms until they are golden color. Remove the mushrooms with a slotted spoon and add them to the frypan with the rabbit pieces and onion. Combine the onion soup mix with the bouillon and pour it over the rabbit pieces. Spoon the sour cream over all the ingredients in the frypan. Cover the pan and simmer for 1 hour, or until the rabbit is tender, occasionally spooning the sauce in the pan over the rabbit. Serve with hot brown rice.

Serves 4.

VENISON

To ensure proper butchering of your deer, take it to a professional butcher. The basic cuts of deer are similar to beef:

1. Loin: choice roasts or steaks (similar to sirloin or porterhouse).

2. Rump: good for pot roast and ground meat.

3. Round: good steaks.

4. Shank, Neck, Flank: soups and stews (cut into cubes or ground up). If the butcher removes all the tendons, the neck makes a good roast.

5. Shoulder: pot roast.

6. Ribs: excellent barbecued or baked (similar to spareribs).

The clue to success in deer handling is the removal of all bones and fat since the gamy flavor is concentrated in these areas. Have your butcher cut scrap meat off the bones and discard the bones. Also, cut away and discard all white (fat) areas. The bloodshot meat and areas with tissue broken from the impact of the bullet should also be discarded. Place all scrap meats and lesser cuts in a pile to be ground into hamburger or made into salami or sausage.

If you plan to oven-roast the less choice cuts of venison, have your butcher lard the meat or you can tie a thin strip of salt pork or lay a few strips of bacon over the roast to ensure its juiciness.

Pan-Fried Venison

4 venison steaks,
   approximately ¼ inch
   thick
Butter

Venison Sauce:
1 cup currant jelly
2 beef bouillon cubes

1 tablespoon butter
¾ cup Burgundy wine

Fry the venison in a small amount of butter, just as you would a steak. When done, remove the venison to a hot platter. Leave the drippings in the skillet and add the sauce ingredients. Allow the liquid to come to a boil, stirring constantly. Pour the sauce over venison.

Serves 4.

Mighty Tasty Marinated Venison Steaks

6 venison steaks
1½ cups dry red wine
   (Burgundy)
½ cup wine vinegar
¾ cup olive oil
2 garlic cloves, minced
   on grater

1 tablespoon fresh onion,
   minced on grater
1 bay leaf, crushed
Sage, salt, and pepper to
   taste

Combine all the above ingredients (except the venison) in a large pan. Add the steaks and marinate for 6 hours in the refrigerator. If the venison steaks are frozen, you do not have to defrost them before marinating. Increase the marinating time by at least 2 hours.

To cook: Barbecue the steaks on a grill over very hot coals for about 4 minutes per side for medium-rare meat. Or place the steaks under the broiler. Baste with the marinade.

Serves 4 to 6.

Sliced Venison Steak with Peppers

3 venison steaks, sliced
  into 1-inch-thick strips
2 tablespoons butter
2 tablespoons cooking oil
3 green peppers, sliced
  into 1-inch-thick strips

1 large onion, diced
1 garlic clove, crushed
1/4 teaspoon salt
1/4 teaspoon pepper

Combine the butter and oil in a large frypan. Add the green peppers, onion, garlic, salt, and pepper. Sauté until the peppers and onion are soft. Push the vegetables to the side of the pan, add the venison strips, and quickly brown them on all sides. Stir all the ingredients together in a pan, cook for 5 minutes, and serve immediately. Hot white rice and escalloped apples are a nice accompaniment to this dish.

Serves 4.

Whiskey-Marinated Venison

1 hindquarter venison

Whiskey Marinade:
1 cup whiskey
6 whole peppercorns
1/2 teaspoon celery seeds
3 tablespoons
  concentrated liquid

garlic
12-ounce can
  concentrated orange
  juice

Combine the marinade ingredients in a large pan. Put the venison in a pan, spoon marinade on top, cover, and refrigerate for 24 to 36 hours, occasionally turning the meat in the marinade.

Lightly oil the barbecue grill and place the meat on top of the grill. Baste the venison with marinade at 15-minute intervals. Turn the meat after 1/2 hour. Barbecue for another 30 minutes.

Serves 6.

Venison Stew

3 pounds venison, cut
  into 2-inch cubes
2 cups dry red wine
¼ cup olive oil
4 tablespoons vinegar
6 peppercorns
2 garlic cloves, crushed
1 bay leaf, crushed
4 tablespoons flour
¼ pound salt pork, diced
3 cups beef bouillon
2 teaspoons Worces-
tershire sauce
Salt, pepper, and garlic
  powder to taste
18 tiny whole onions,
  peeled
2 carrots, cut in 1-inch
  rounds
½ cup sautéed
  mushrooms
2 potatoes, cut into 6
  pieces each
½ cup sherry

Combine the wine, olive oil, vinegar, peppercorns, garlic, and bay leaf in a large bowl. Place the venison cubes in the bowl. Cover and refrigerate for 24 hours, turning the meat in the marinade once or twice. After 24 hours, remove the cubes from the marinade. Strain the marinade and reserve ¼ cup for the sauce.

Lightly dust the venison with flour. In a large frypan, sauté the salt pork until golden. Add the venison and brown on all sides. Meanwhile, in a separate pot, bring the bouillon—mixed with the reserved marinade and Worcestershire sauce—to a boil. Pour off the fat drippings accumulated in the frypan. Slowly add the boiling bouillon mixture to the meat, stirring to blend the flour bits sticking to the bottom of the pan (from venison) into the sauce. Season to taste with salt, pepper, and garlic powder. Add all the vegetables and bring to a boil. Cover, reduce the heat, and gently simmer for 1 hour, stirring occasionally. Add the sherry, stir, and cover. Cook for another 15 minutes, or until the meat is tender.

Serves 6 to 8.

This is Bill's favorite. It is similar to a Mexican chili.

Green's Groudo

1 1/2 pounds ground
  venison
Cooking oil
1 large garlic clove,
  chopped
1 onion, coarsely
  chopped
Salt and pepper
8-ounce can tomato sauce
3 medium tomatoes,
  peeled and chopped
15-ounce can pinto or red
  beans
3-ounce can chopped
  chile peppers or 4
  small fresh yellow
  chile peppers, diced
1/2 teaspoon chili powder
3 stalks celery, coarsely
  chopped (optional)

Crumble the venison with your hands and sauté it in oil with the garlic and onion until the onion is golden. Season with salt and pepper. Add the tomato sauce, tomatoes, beans, chile peppers, and chili powder. Stir thoroughly to mix all the ingredients. Simmer, covered, for 45 minutes, occasionally stirring. Add the celery for a crunchy texture and simmer, uncovered, for 6 minutes. If it is too thick, add a small amount of water. Serve it piping hot with Mexican flour or corn tortillas. Excellent frozen and reheated.

Serves 2 to 4.

Index